CARING
MINISTRY

CARING
MINISTRY

A Contemplative Approach
to Pastoral Care

Sarah A. Butler

CONTINUUM • NEW YORK

1999

The Continuum Publishing Company
370 Lexington Avenue, New York, NY 10017

Printed in the United States of America

Library of Congress Cataloging-in-Publication Data
Butler, Sarah A.
  Caring ministry : a contemplative approach to pastoral care /
  Sarah A. Butler.
    p. cm.
  Includes bibliographical references.
  ISBN 0-8264-1159-2
  1. Pastoral psychology. 2. Contemplation. 3. Church work.
I. Title.
BV4012.B89   1999
253.5'2 – dc21   98-51343
                                                        CIP

Contents

Acknowledgments

I want to express my deep appreciation to the community who helped give birth to this text. Canon David Morgan, Margaret Johnson, and Diane Smith, who have assisted me in teaching the Caring Ministry program also provided valuable input and suggestions. Diane Smith collaborated with me on "Understanding Loss, Grief, and Death." None of this could have come about without the computer wizardry of Robert Francisco, who spent countless hours interpreting my handwriting. My thanks go to the staff of St. John's Episcopal Cathedral and especially to the Very Reverend Charles E. Kiblinger for making writing time possible. And finally I want to thank all the caring ministers at St. John's for receiving this material and claiming their own gifts of ministry.

Introduction

"Do not be afraid, little flock, for it is your Father's good plea-sure to give you the kingdom.... Make purses for yourselves that do not wear out, an unfailing treasure in heaven, where no thief comes near and no moth destroys. For where your treasure is, there your heart will be also."   (Luke 12:32–34)

In this world of fast food, microwaves, seven-second commercials, e-mail, high stress jobs, cell phones, and superhighways, one of the best gifts we can offer each other is a listening heart. Many of us already regard ourselves as good listeners, until, that is, we are challenged to observe our own responses and attentiveness.

To listen to another is to carve out a safe sacred space where we encounter the mystery of suffering in another human being. This in-deed is a journey of courage that requires of us some preparation and fortification. If we are to become effective caregivers, we need to fill our purses with that which does not wear out and with that which will serve us and others in this continuation of Christ's ministry.

We take a step of faith each time we walk into the hospital room or the grief-stricken home. We do not know what we will find, but God has gone before us and is already at work creating a space for healing. Just as the spiritual director learns that his or her primary function is "not to get in the way," the pastoral caregiver learns that a vital piece of ministry is to discern when *not* to speak. The awe-filled posture toward the other often requires less articulation and fewer words on our part rather than more. Our ability to listen and to set aside our compulsion to share what's on our minds reveals our willingness to cooperate with the movement of the Holy Spirit and to trust God's healing presence.

Caring ministry is about what we know *and* who we are. We share the fruit of our intimate relationship with Christ. Our cultivation of listening, awe-filled prayer nurtures our capacity to listen to one who is hurting.

I know of no better way to cultivate this receptive posture toward others than to practice by listening to God. It is through some form of faithful silent prayer that the contemplative dimension deepens, is exercised, and becomes second nature for the pastoral caregiver. Freed from the constant need to talk at people (or God) we move to the contemplative space of being present to the story and the feelings, thus allowing the encounter to be transformed into Holy Ground.

Just what do I mean by contemplative? For me to be a contemplative is to look at life in a way that savors God's divine influence in all things. It is acting in accordance with "God's good pleasure to give us the kingdom" and to cease to react out of our cultural assumptions or our fear, pain, or anger. Contemplatives give themselves to an encounter for the sheer joy or appreciation or delight or love of it and without analysis, for example:

- sitting with a dying friend or relative, holding her hand and listening to the shallow breaths as if each one were a prayer,

- listening to a symphony and allowing the vibrations to speak to our souls,

- sensing God's goodness and yearning for our reception of grace even in the midst of trials and confusion,

and my favorite:

- holding an infant, making that eye contact that begins a dialogue of animated expressions, goos, coos, giggles, kisses, funny noises and faces, even a few "sacred words" — but no paragraphs please.

There are many ways to cultivate contemplative listening and living. One that stands out as tried and true and accessible to all Christians is the Centering Prayer method (see the Appendix for Thomas Keating's explanation). It is so simple that we try to make it harder than it really is. The practice of Centering Prayer offers a structure for us to enter into a prayer that is often dormant in our traditions. As we hear the words "be still then, and know that I am God" (Ps. 46:11), we may wonder how. Centering Prayer provides a space and a discipline for the "still" prayer of praise and adoration. We sit in silence, we choose a "sacred word" which symbolizes our intention simply to enjoy God's presence. When we become aware of distractions, we return gently to the "sacred word," and at the conclusion of the prayer time we sit in silence for a couple of minutes.

Those simple motions draw us into a prayer of deep dialogue where God speaks and we listen, not with the mind but in the deepest part of our being. We rest from the usual monologue of our verbal prayers, and we acknowledge God's capacity to speak to us in a "still small voice."

In order to allow a rich dialogue to take place in ministry, the pastoral caregiver must do as we do in Centering Prayer even when it feels as if we are just going through the motions. As we listen to a care receiver we go through some of those same steps:

- We sit in silence, for the most part, with the intention of listening to the other's story.

- When thoughts arise about ourselves ("her mother's death reminds me of the difficult time I had when my mom died"), we return, ever so gently, to the "sacred story" of the person in front of us.

- We let go of our own distractions ("I need to stop at the office and then pick up my son") and return to the "sacred story."

- We let go of reactions, judgments, analysis, and return to the "sacred story."

- We have some form of closing prayer with the care receiver.

You may notice the thoughts, distractions, reactions, and solutions that flow across your stream of consciousness as you listen. But try to save them for your own private reflection time and ask how God may be speaking to you in them.

Although the guidelines for Centering Prayer and pastoral care don't have strict parallels, I hope you can connect the two and appreciate the value of your intention to listen, to be open, and to love as Christ has loved us.

_હ. *Chapter 1*

Pastoral Care as Contemplative Journey*

Beloved, let us love one another, because love is from God; every-one who loves is born of God and knows God. . . . In this is love, not that we loved God, but that he loved us and sent his Son to be the atoning sacrifice for our sins. Beloved, since God loved us so much, we also ought to love one another. No one has ever seen God; if we love one another, God lives in us, and his love is perfected in us. (1 John 4:7, 10–12)

I arrived at the Intensive Care Unit feeling helpless and hopeless. Patti had already been pronounced dead once. She had suffered an unexplainable spontaneous bleeding of the spinal column. Later she would remember trying to scream to the doctor that she was alive, but she couldn't force out the words. Her chances were now considered slim. What could I possibly do? All my skills and knowledge seemed inadequate in the face of Patti's emotional tidal wave. Her physical pain was accompanied by the deepest emotional wailing I'd ever encountered. I wanted to flee from the scene of a soul left raw and assaulted by every imaginable fear. "Patti, I am so sorry. What can I do for you?" With a beseeching moan, she replied, "Love me, just love me!" With a grateful sigh I answered, "That I can do." Her simple plea summoned me to the heart and core of all pastoral care: love as Christ loves us. In the ensuing days, I merely sat with Patti, allowing my presence to be her reassurance of God's love. Months would go by before she needed to talk about her experience and sort through the barrage of feelings.

---

*Much of this chapter was taken from Sarah A. Butler, "Pastoral Care and Centering Prayer," in *Centering Prayer in Daily Life and Ministry*, ed. Thomas Keating and Gustave Reininger (New York: Continuum, 1998).

There is a dimension of caring not enjoyed by the other helping professions that leaves us free and engaged in ministry when it appears we are doing nothing. At its center, pastoral care is a contemplative posture: "Love me, just love me." We are seldom solving, curing, or changing; rather, we are simply encountering the other person's pain with an attitude of faith and reliance on the relationship we share with Christ.

Could we not borrow Patti's words to sum up the mutual attraction in prayer? God's plea of the ages has been for creatures to respond in love with a passion that supersedes any circumstances. And if we were to strip away all our motives in prayer, all wishes, thoughts, distractions, plans, complaints, might we also crave some time to sit with God and whisper, "Just love me?"

The substance of the contemplative relationship is love and union, but it has a variety of methods or structures that release its grace. The Jesus prayer, the Ignatian Exercises, and the Daily Office are but a few such forms. I highlight the method of Centering Prayer, an ancient tradition adapted for our time by Thomas Keating, Basil Pennington, and William Meninger. The simplicity of Centering Prayer makes it accessible for lay people to appropriate as a daily discipline. I have witnessed many lay people training for pastoral ministry who embrace the practice of Centering Prayer as a means of nurturing their own faith. I believe there is a subconscious attraction to Centering Prayer and praying with Scripture (*lectio divina,* from which it derives) because they share the fundamental elements and rhythms of effective pastoral care. Or perhaps it is because effective pastoral care mirrors the full range of prayer, from active and attentive modalities to resting in God's presence. I identify these rhythms and elements as (1) divine/human collaboration (2) care and prayer as relationship, and (3) the parallel dynamics of *lectio divina* and pastoral care.

Divine/Human Collaboration

A recurring theme throughout this book is the recollection of who we are and who God is. In pastoral situations we sometimes pray for God's intervention as though God were blissfully unaware of the crises and required our supplications. However, God is already active in the hearts and lives of both care receiver and caregiver long before the faintest whisper of need and longing. Our prayers should not be an alarm for God's attention but a request to participate in God's healing process. Indeed, we function best as pastors when we recognize that we are a part of a process greater than our efforts, which is the healing that God has initiated. If we, like the disciples, presume that feeding the five thousand rests on our shoulders alone, what hope do we have? However, like the lad in the Gospel story who humbly offers his little cache of five loaves and two fishes to Jesus to help feed the five thousand, we are quickly relieved to see that all we can offer is just our presence and compassion. God does the rest, responding with the divine surprise, using our limited offerings to effect great works.

In Centering Prayer we are drawn into the same divine/human collaboration. The efficacy of prayer does not rest with us but with God. We need only consent to the presence and action of God within us. The practice of Centering Prayer calls for a silent receptivity, a "letting go" of control ("I'm divine") or of notions about how God should respond (God as efficient secretary). This prayer of silence and letting go is a deep confirmation of our trust in the strength of the Lord. Do we believe that God is capable of responding only when we do the talking? Or does prayer also include a time of listening? In prayer, listening rather than talking or asking can be a surrender to the mystery and wisdom that our eyes, ears, and intellect cannot access (1 Cor. 2:7–10). Indeed, Centering Prayer is defined by its proponent Thomas Keating as a method that facilitates contemplative prayer, which he describes as: "the opening of mind and heart.... Moved by God's sustaining grace, we open our awareness to God, who we know by faith is within us, closer than breathing, closer than thinking, closer than consciousness itself."*

It is from this privileged place within us where the Spirit dwells, where we access and receive Holy Wisdom (Rom. 8:26–27), that the Spirit flows outward through our gifts into the tangible world. The rhythms of Centering Prayer — from knowing to unknowing, from

---

*Thomas Keating, *Intimacy with God* (New York: Crossroad, 1995), 41.

doing to being, from information to formation, from context to contemplation — renew the wonder and awe that keep us ever mindful
of God at the center of the pastoral care relationship.

In our daily life this spiritual attentiveness to God's living presence
can cause a fundamental shift in our self-identity — from knowing to
unknowing, from the certainty of our needs to the infinity of pastoral
needs to which God ministers. Analogously, over 450 years ago the
universe was thought to revolve around the earth. Humankind, master of earth, was the center of creation. The Copernican discovery
that the universe did not revolve around the earth caused a cata-
clysmic shift in human consciousness. Now science tells us that the
universe, born of infinite energy, is still expanding and moving. Our
earth-centered consciousness has given way to a vision of an infinite
universe; similarly, our ego-centered consciousness can strive toward
the infinity of union with the divine.

In Centering Prayer, as in the pastoral relationship, we may begin
with our projections or with other gods such as superstitions, personal whims, or ignorance. All of these drain our spiritual energies.
If we can listen and allow God's initiative to spark the fire of love, we
can go beyond word, thought, and emotion — beyond verbal, mental,
and affective prayer — to the awe of God without limits. Humility
blossoms as we realize it will take an eternity to fathom the depths of
God's love. Certainly, this is what St. John of the Cross meant when he
sighed that we are all beginners.* Indeed, the metaphor becomes reality as that humble posture of openness to God's unfolding presence
reveals a place of unknowing where mystery and matter meet.

Care and Prayer as Relationship

A second striking parallel between pastoral care and the practice of
Centering Prayer is a common call to relationship. Pastoral caregivers should quickly learn that they are not in the business of
solving problems. They must learn instead to place emphasis on developing a caring relationship and becoming a supporting presence.

---

*See *The Collected Works of St. John of the Cross*, trans. Kieran Kavanaugh and Otilio
Rodriguez (Washington, D.C.: ICS Publications, 1991), vol. 2, chapter 12, "The Ascent of
Mount Carmel."

Though there may be many healing results from careful listening and respectful presence, expectations should always rest on offering up the outcome to God's love.

Pastoral care naturally begins in dialogue. An intimacy and comfort in the relationship develop that can embrace prayerful silence. Though this cannot be rushed, it can be nurtured by a full acceptance of the care receiver's story. Such acceptance often is sensed as a permission to let go of anxiety and worry about the future and rest in the caregiver's presence as a witness to God's hope.

Like pastoral care, the relationship of prayer generally begins in dialogue. Whether we pray with the Scriptures or by speaking directly with God, we begin in an individual context as we express our needs of petition, intercession, penitence, and oblation. These expressions make possible the unfolding of our story and God's place in it. They are essential steps in the development of a full relationship with God. Many Christians, though, never go beyond these more active modalities of prayer. Many never enter into any regular practice of adoration "asking nothing but to enjoy God's presence."*

I've used the word "dialogue" to refer to prayer in its discursive and verbal expressions. I would like to challenge the reader to scrutinize these expressions to determine whether they are dialogue or monologue. For the less mature or the spiritual tourist prayer can easily stall in a one-sided monologue. If our prayers remain on the level of "Take away my pain," "Help me find a job," "Lead me to a good parking space downtown," they may be only wishes to conform God to our particular needs.

But the very same utterances can be the beginning of a rich dialogue if we welcome the Spirit to interact with us. Confirmation of true dialogue is our willingness to listen to God's self-disclosure. For instance, I might include Emily, who has cancer, in my daily intercessions without really engaging my heart and mind with her situation. But if I cultivate an honest dialogue with God about Emily, I might uncover my own anger at God for not preventing or intervening in her illness. If I go deeper I risk touching my own brokenness. Further in and deeper still and I discover God's broken heart for Emily and her family. This could open up reflections on the suffering Christ

---

*The Book of Common Prayer (New York: Church Hymnal Corp., 1979), 847.

or new insights into God's love and goodness or give way to holy tears. The fruit of such interaction may be a prompting to minister to Emily with an unexplained peace. I have been drawn into God's longing love for her. What could have remained a monologue has become a dialogue.

We must begin with prayer as the expression of our needs, but we must go further. We must allow our prayers to unfold, to draw us out of ourselves into the heart of faith where mere words cannot communicate. As the prayer of God's presence develops, we become less dependent on language and eventually surrender to the silent mystery of God's "real presence." The method of Centering Prayer enables the unfolding movement from the more verbal modes of prayer to the silence of contemplative prayer.

Centering Prayer does not depend on our moods, distractions, or fatigue; it does, however, rely upon our unrelenting intention to be with God. We discover that even in sitting to begin our practice we are more than the sum of our distractions. Centering Prayer bids us beyond the context of our thoughts (no matter how collected or frazzled), beyond our feelings (no matter how tranquil or distraught), beyond all selfish concerns into the contemplative dimension of naked, loving presence. The silence nurtures us mysteriously. We return to our daily lives restored, strengthened, and peaceful — not because we seek this in our prayers but because we only seek God and God seeks us. It is not the subjective experience in prayer, ranging from tranquillity to incessant distraction, but our intention of consent to God's presence and action within that transforms us.

C. S. Lewis in *The Screwtape Letters* casts this issue in a simple prose paradigm: Screwtape often advises Wormwood to teach his human to analyze the value of his prayers in terms of the feelings they produce and to judge the success of prayer as being wholly dependent on the human's state of being at the moment of prayer. His devilish advice was to keep all prayer subjective and to fix one's longing gaze on one's self rather than on God.*

---

*C. S. Lewis, *The Screwtape Letters* (New York: Macmillan, 1961), 16, 20, and elsewhere.

Likewise, in pastoral care we resist the temptation to judge a care visit by its perceived success or failure. We never know what seeds are planted by our words and acts of compassion. This, too is a consent of faith in God, who embraces all things and events in love. The contemplative pastor is at ease in allowing God to be divine rather than adopting that impossible role for ourselves.

The Parallel Dynamics of *Lectio Divina* and Pastoral Care

The rhythms of *lectio divina* and effective pastoral care are strikingly clear. *Lectio divina* is the Christian contemplative tradition's way of reading and praying with the Holy Scriptures. It leads one into deeper relationship and, ultimately, contemplative union with God. Distilled from *lectio divina*, the method of Centering Prayer attempts to facilitate the transition from the active modes of prayer, from mental and affective prayer (*meditatio* and *oratio*), to the silent, awe-filled prayer of presence (*contemplatio*). An established practice of Centering Prayer enriches the practice of *lectio divina*.

Lectio divina begins in reading and reflecting. From there it moves into a dialogue with God and our emotional responses. It eventually ends with our resting in the silence of divine presence. This movement echoes the rhythms of pastoral care. Out of this "conversation," through which we learn the care receiver's story emerges the intimacy that allows self-disclosure. The dynamic of intimacy and self-disclosure allows caregivers to move into the peace where they can offer a quiet presence, the contemplative dimension of caregiving.

Another striking comparison between *lectio divina* and pastoral care is the value of the repetition of the story. One reading of Scripture is simply inadequate to uncover the reflections and responses that can be elicited from the text. Likewise, those who have undergone a crisis need to be able to repeat their account of the event over and over again. This repetition first allows what seemed impossible to begin to become real. As the story continues to be retold, nuances are noticed that will become a part of one's sacred story. Healing takes place as both caregiver and care receiver express multiple feelings, ask difficult questions, and listen to God's call to reorder that which was in disorder. In time, the need to know all the answers gives way to faith and an appreciation of God's sustaining grace.

Consider the parallels between the dynamics of *lectio divina* and those of pastoral care, as shown below.

Lectio Divina	Pastoral Care Ministry
Read the story in God's Word (lectio): Be present to the Word. Listen to the story for information. Take it in. Get acquainted with the passage of Scripture.	*Listen to the care receiver's story:* Be present to the person. Listen to the story for information. Receive it nonjudgmentally. Get acquainted with the person.
Reflect (meditatio): Become actively involved with the story. *Pay attention to what attracts your attention.* Notice your own feelings. Reflect on your own inner experience of the Scripture. Allow the Gospels to be a mirror of your own life.	*Reflect:* Focus on the feelings. *Pay attention to what attracts your attention.* Begin to see the unique person that God loves. Recognize and accept the person's inner experience. Mirror back your perception of the care receiver's inner experience.
Respond (oratio): Be free to express what is pouring out of the reflection: praise, tears, repentance, thanksgiving, etc. How is God becoming formed in you? Celebrate this with thanksgiving.	*Respond:* Allow the person to respond to the mirroring above — with tears, insight, experience, repentance, thanksgiving, etc. Celebrate this with thanksgiving.
Rest (contemplatio): Let go of all reflections and responses in order to allow God to speak to you in the mystery of silence and quiet presence. Surrender to the mystery and awe.	*Rest:* Let go of the need to know the outcome. Offer prayer, silence, or just your presence. This is the contemplative dimension of caring. Sit in awe of God's divine action in the other.

Life crises or painful events plunge us into the reality of our human frailty. They represent a ripe opportunity to offer our helplessness as the context in which God's healing grace can be initiated. When we are the most empty and confused, our greatest need is the presence of someone who cares. The caring priest or lay minister must not arrive armed with answers but with faith and the courage simply to be mindfully present to someone in pain. Similarly, we must not arrive in prayer with an agenda of wants, needs, and directives for how God should respond. Often, it is precisely because life crises underscore our inability to order and control our world that these events become turning points The reordering process, or transformation, is an invitation to the discovery of divine surprise in all of life. Likewise, a regular practice of Centering Prayer also draws us into our deepest place of emptiness; it is an acknowledgment that we cannot completely control and order our lives, that we are wholly dependent on God. It is our consent that opens a space for God's reordering of our lives, that allows a transformation to take place.

All pastors, lay or clergy, can learn valuable skills and benefit immeasurably from mutual ministry support activities. Our experiences at the Cathedral of St. John in Denver have led us to make available not only pastoral care but also programs of Centering Prayer and *lectio divina* as means of exploring the divine/human collaboration. This approach enables us to receive our ministry as a gift and as an invitation to share in Christ's larger ministry of divine union with us all.

The Role of the Caregiver

You yourselves are our letter, written on our hearts, to be known and read by all; and you show that you are a letter of Christ, prepared by us, written not with ink but with the Spirit of the living God, not on tablets of stone but on tablets of human hearts.

Such is the confidence that we have through Christ toward God. Not that we are competent of ourselves to claim anything as coming from us; our competence is from God, who has made us competent to be ministers of a new covenant, not of letter but of spirit; for the letter kills, but the Spirit gives life.

(2 Cor. 3:2–6)

The biggest temptation for pastoral caregivers is the belief that we are there to solve a problem, to give an answer, or to "fix it." This is a natural human reaction since it enables us to feel useful, and it lessens the uncomfortable feeling generated from seeing someone else in pain. Throughout this book you will be examining and learning a model of ministry that will help you to disentangle your own needs from those of your care receiver and that will present a biblical model of compassion, freedom, right use of gifts, and nonjudgmental support.

Each chapter is designed to reinforce the primary role of the caring minister as offering a supportive presence — to be, as it were, the "letter of Christ." Even the most experienced pastors need to recall that they are God's instruments of love and not the Master Musician. In this model of pastoral care the development of the caring relationship rather than the end result is emphasized. To begin our introduction to this model, let us borrow a device used by the corporate world to define roles: the job description.

Job Descriptions: Human and Divine*

My experience has taught me that the most effective pastoral care-givers are those who humbly and consciously recognize that their ministry — from intention to effect — is a gift from God. However, even the most gifted caregivers among us can get so caught up in the activity and importance of our enterprise that we forget this larger view of our ministry. Indeed, it is easy to fall into the subtle seduction of doing too many good works on the power of our own talent and strength. I know I have fallen into this trap and have found myself talking to God in prayer as I would instruct an efficient secretary to organize my calendar, carry out my delegated requests, and act as a buffer for those annoying interruptions that thwart my ministry and my life. When I catch myself doing this, I try to remember what part of pastoral care is my responsibility and what part God directs.

Foolhardy as it may seem, I have written job descriptions for the caregiver, for the care receiver, and for God, a divine/human collaboration of sorts (see the chart on the following page). Reading these whimsical job descriptions almost always jolts me back from feeling that the whole task rests with me or that I have a monopoly on God's services.

God does a far superior job of sticking to this plan than the caregiver. When we find our ministry off center, it is because we sometimes operate as if God were human and we were divine. We notice this most as a lack of joy and soon find ourselves in need of a moment of remembrance, a call to wonder, to see that it is God who initiates and we who respond.

You may be wondering why the caregiver is needed if it is God who is ultimately responsible for an outcome of healing and wholeness. The entire Judeo-Christian story is one of the reception of God's grace by and through members of the faith community. All Christians are called to be co-creators, ambassadors, and participants in the Lord's activity, and the caregiver is acting in this capacity.

---

*Parts of this chapter are taken from Sarah A. Butler, "Pastoral Care and Centering Prayer," in *Centering Prayer in Daily Life and Ministry*, ed. Thomas Keating and Gustave Reininger (New York: Continuum, 1998).

JOB DESCRIPTIONS

CARING MINISTERS	CARE RECEIVERS*	GOD
To be human: to embrace our human role; to respond in humility, knowing that we cannot see the future or be certain of what is best, but we can consent to God's grace at work; to use and recognize our own gifts.	**To be human:** to embrace our human role; to respond with the humble posture that we do not walk this path alone but need the support of our faith community to receive God's grace.	**To be divine:** to know the best thing and the best mode of healing; to initiate the caring relationship.
To listen: to offer the rare gift of being attentive and unafraid of another's pain.	To share their story	**To be active:** to be involved in each individual story as much as in the rich tradition of the Judeo-Christian story.
To focus on feelings: to reach beneath the superficial and appreciate the rich depths of the care receiver.	To risk sharing feelings	**To be ultimately responsible:** to bring about the healing that mends the broken heart and leads people forward.
To offer a supportive presence: to simply be there to offer "unconditional positive regard" (Carl Rogers) or, better, "to abide in awe-filled attention" (Adrian Van Kaam).	**To consent:** to accept God's grace by being willing to change, grow, and accept healing.	**To be constant and faithful:** to be full of surprises in this caring relationship.
To share faith, hope, and love: to let the Holy Spirit work as appropriate.	**To experience God's activity:** to let the Holy Spirit work in their lives in a new way.	**To give grace:** to help when people need help.

*All optional. Only the care receiver can make the choices.

Consequences of Exceeding Job Description Boundaries

When the caring minister attempts to take on the responsibility of the care receiver or of God, the following may occur:

Anger. The minister feels anger toward the care receiver for not responding to all the effort and energy the minister has contributed to the relationship.

Microwave Expectations. The minister is impatient, wanting to see immediate results and not respecting that healing takes time. Compare in your own mind the difference in taste between a pre-packaged cup of soup "zapped" in the microwave and a pot of homemade soup put together from scratch and simmered for hours. There is no comparison. Microwave ministry may have some limited value just as soup in a paper cup is better than none. The patient pastor will allow time for "simmering."

Exhaustion. A Nebraska farmer (also claimed by Iowa, Kansas, and Ohio) once said, "Don't try to teach a pig to sing; it will wear you out and just annoy the pig." If the pastor approaches the care receiver armed with good advice, pat answers, and, worst of all, the desire to make the care receiver feel good, it will usually result in an irritated care receiver and a tired caring minister. When ministers forget the divine role of God, they can fall into the trap of depending on their own power alone. This "messiah complex" is evidenced as the ministers exhaust themselves in doing too many "good works." The weight of doing it all is crushing.

Withdrawal. People often withdraw from those who are in great pain because they feel helpless to "fix it." I remember visiting a woman in the hospital who had fallen into a semi-coma. As I stood by the bed, she regained consciousness for a few minutes and said, "I'm dying, aren't I?" I asked her, "What makes you think you're dying?" "Because they aren't working on me anymore," was her answer. She was exactly right. In the previous days, she had been rushed to emergency surgery and taken to various parts of the hospital for test after test. She was constantly surrounded by medical personnel, and her room was filled with all sorts of monitoring and life-saving equipment. When it became clear that nothing was going to save her life, all equipment was withdrawn (appropriate in her case), and medical personnel became scarce. Since it was their job to "fix it" and "it" was hopeless, they withdrew their presence.

The role of the pastoral caregiver is quite different. We acknowledge our helplessness to fix what is broken and therefore are left free to provide a loving, caring presence even in an outwardly hopeless situation. Caring ministers who remain clear about their job descriptions will not withdraw from an individual in pain. Our very presence is an affirmation and belief that the divine mystery continues to operate in and through human weakness.

Other feelings such as discouragement or low self-esteem may crop up if we attempt to bear the burden of God's job. What we do offer, along with sound skills, is our *intention,* born out of our desire to be compassionate, caring, and united in love to another Christian who is hurting. Our intention to offer pastoral care is identical to our intention to be united in love with God through Centering Prayer: *just being there.* This posture is humorously captured by comedian Woody Allen's statement in the film *Annie Hall:* "Ninety-six percent of success is just showing up." How many prophets in the First Testament tried to refuse God's call with excuses: "I'm too old"; "I'm too young"; "Nobody will listen"; or — even more terrifying — "What happens if they *do* listen?" God's response to almost every prophet's reticence, however, is, "Just show up. I'll do the rest; you'll be amazed at the results. You be human. I'll be divine."

Many pastors responding to crises — perhaps feeling exhausted or irritated at the time — have discovered with some amazement that it was their mere presence that served as the catalyst for bringing God's compassion and healing into a difficult situation. God somehow uses our willingness just to "show up," our humble part of the divine/human collaboration, as the yeast or lump of clay, the last ounce of oil and flour to make a miracle. Intention in pastoral care can sometimes be all, eclipsing even the best skill, training, and professionalism.

Conclusion

Finally, as you begin to focus on process over outcomes, you will discover that the greatest gift you have to offer as a caregiver is to be a vessel through whom the Holy Spirit can operate. You will be a source for healing to the extent that you are able *to set aside your own agenda.*

When Herb O'Driscoll was teaching a group of clergy how to preach more effectively, he pointed out the most important "skill" of a good preacher: "What people really long for in the pulpit is to be in the presence of a man or woman of faith."* We can apply that same statement to the caring minister as well. What people in pain truly long for is to be in the presence of a man or woman of faith, a person who truly believes that God can and will help.

You will indeed acquire helpful skills and learn new competencies, but, more importantly, you have the opportunity of becoming greater men and women of faith. Here are some Scripture passages you might read using the *lectio divina* form of prayer. They reinforce the different dynamics at work in the pastoral relationship and the divine/human collaboration.

John 3:30 (John the Baptist declares): "He must increase, but I must decrease."

Philippians 4:13: "I can do all things through him who strengthens me."

2 Corinthians 5:19–21: "In Christ God was reconciling the world to himself . . . and *entrusting the message of reconciliation to us.* So we are *ambassadors* for Christ, since God is making his appeal through us; we entreat you on behalf of Christ, be reconciled to God."

Spiritual Application

Read 1 Kings 17:8–16. Take a few minutes and reflect on this striking example of the divine/human collaboration.

- How did Elijah demonstrate humility and faith?
- How did the widow take a risk?
- How did God fulfill the divine role?

In this touching story, we observe the movement from fear and despair to a sense of family and faith. We may think it odd that

---

*From a lecture at the College of Preachers, Washington, D.C., April 1989.

Elijah requested of the widow the very little that she possessed. The prophet invited her to give him all she had: her poverty, loneliness, despair, and pain. The widow took a risk and revealed her intention to give up and die along with her son. Elijah declared, "Do not be afraid," offering his supportive presence, his intention to be obedient to this call, and the opportunity to become family. God was faithful and transformed their emptiness and fear but also their willingness to consent into a life-saving miracle.

In addition to our intentions, skills, and our humble dependence on God, we have acquired a personal integrity rooted in our own experience. We have each developed a wisdom from losses, struggles, and crises, endowing our ministry with sensitivity. Remember a time of turmoil in your own life and reflect upon its influence:

- Was someone present to you? What did that person's presence mean to you?

- What do you wish that person had done differently?

- Were you alone? What feelings can you identify as you faced the crisis by yourself?

- How were you ultimately sustained? by God? others? self?

The Gift of Listening

O Lord, you have searched me and known me.
You know when I sit down and when I rise up;
You discern my thoughts from far away.
You search out my path and my lying down,
and are acquainted with all my ways.
Even before a word is on my tongue,
O Lord, you know it completely.

(Ps. 139:1–4)

Only God knows what I think and feel "even before a word is on my tongue." Yet even God draws us into dialogue for the sake of the relationship and to unearth thoughts and feelings we may have not yet recognized. To learn to listen to others, we can begin with an exercise in listening to ourselves.

Before proceeding any further, take a few minutes to place your hearts and minds in a posture of listening. Get as comfortable as you are able in your chair with both feet on the floor, eyes closed, and back straight. Read the following guided meditation and allow it to create openness and receptivity:

> You may have had a day filled with too many obligations packed into too few hours. We all suffer from the effects of a culture that seems to insist that we live our lives motivated by the four-letter word *BUSY*. All of us find ourselves, at one time or another, too busy to allow sufficient time to care for ourselves and others or to invite God to nurture us with healing love. As you sit quietly, place your hands on your knees with palms facing up. This symbolizes the release of all the cares and stresses of the day. As they rise before you, release them to God's love and control. Likewise, recall the joys that graced

your day, no matter how small. As they rise in your memory offer them back to God with a prayer of thanksgiving. In the next two minutes of silence let go of any external or internal distractions that may impede your ability to listen to God, to your companions in this life, or to the inner responses of your own heart.

> Lord you never cease to listen. Fill us with that same Spirit and grant us the capacity to listen to you, to others, and to ourselves. Amen.

Effective Listening

To truly listen to a person who is undergoing any loss is one of the greatest gifts a caregiver can impart. Some people are naturally good listeners, but most can benefit from reviewing the skills required for attentive listening. Acquiring skills will not be accomplished in one easy lesson. Throughout this book the gift of listening will be reinforced in the content, in the prayer exercises, and in the spiritual applications.

We have identified the ability to listen as a gift, as a grace received from God and in turn offered as a gift to the care receiver. Listening seems to be an increasingly rare activity in our culture. Yet it remains a fairly simple, uncomplicated virtue. Listening affirms our commitment to care and invites people out of their isolation and into community.

When you as a caring minister practice effective listening, you are generously offering the following gifts:

Time. Serious intentional listening takes time. The pastoral caregiver sets aside adequate time to facilitate the process of sharing. Remember the simmering pot: it takes time for the flavors to emerge. Dialogue needs to be interspersed with thoughtful silence. We want to give time, not save time, by cultivating an unhurried atmosphere.

Patience. The caring minister does not rush the process of sharing by reaching a hasty solution, conclusion, judgment, or analysis. We can listen faster than the care receivers can talk. If you find yourself preparing answers while they are still speaking or if you are mentally finishing their sentences, stop, take a deep breath, and let go of any impatience you are feeling.

Confidentiality. The caring minister assures the person that nothing shared will be discussed with or disclosed to others. This is not only a gift but an absolute must. Neither the name nor the details of a caring ministry relationship are revealed to anyone but the supervisor. In a mutual ministry support group, the names of those discussed should be changed.

Respect. It is a gift to have one's uniqueness honored by another. The caring minister offers this respect by valuing the feelings and experience of the care receiver. We put aside our own opinions even in cases where we have undergone a similar experience. Each journey possesses its own character and an individual rhythm for healing.

Energy. Listening is not a passive posture of indifference but an activity that requires one's physical, emotional, and spiritual energy. To be engaged, alert, interested, observant, discerning, and understanding, we need to muster strength from all three energy centers.

Full Attention. Skillful listening embraces all that is said. The gifted listener does not practice selective hearing, which is the tendency to screen out what we do not wish to hear. The minister listens to the whole story without selecting one portion on which to form a conclusion and without discarding information and feelings as unimportant.

Listening as Physical, Emotional, and Spiritual Attentiveness

Physical Attentiveness

We can convey supportive listening through various physical behaviors:

- **Making eye contact.** Eye contact indicates interest, comfort, and care.

- **Posture.** A posture of alertness should be maintained. Leaning forward slightly indicates interest and compassion.

- **Touch.** A gentle touch can communicate a depth and quality of care that even words cannot. Any touch must be appropriate to the situation, for example, frail elderly people often suffer from painful arthritis or fragile thin skin that bruises at the slightest pressure. Be sensitive to the care receiver's comfort level. If your intuition tells you that the care receiver is not a "toucher," obey your instinct.

- **Speech.** Indicate your care with verbal affirmations such as, "Yes, I can hear what you're saying," "Oh, yes?" "I see." Another quality of good listening is the use of Reflective Listening. This will be discussed in more detail in the subsequent chapters. Basically, reflective listening is repeating or reflecting back what has been stated to indicate understanding, acceptance, and encouragement.

There are other indications of our physical attentiveness as well:

- If you need to check the time, look at your watch while you are talking rather than when the care receiver is speaking. It appears less of an interruption if done when the caring minister is speaking.

- Be aware of what your facial expressions are conveying. Nods and smiles, for example, communicate your feelings.

- Allow for short periods of silence. People experiencing emotional pain may need a minute to literally catch their breath or try to get their thoughts straight.

Emotional Attentiveness

The pastoral relationship will naturally require emotional energy as you offer compassion, consideration, care, regard, and vigilance. To listen to another's pain is to extend yourself to another as you courageously acknowledge reality. A skilled caring minister does not withdraw from the person's presence as feelings are disclosed.

Remember, you are not responsible for the care receiver's feelings and therefore not responsible for changing them; only for listening. The empathic listener acts as a companion, as one who offers comfort without allowing the feelings of the care receiver to have a disabling effect on the listener. Empathy gone astray can lead to identification, which is the adoption of another's behavior, values, and feelings. The role of the caring minister is to walk beside a person, not get inside of that person. If the listener overidentifies with the care receiver, confusion sets in. Who is in need of care? Whose journey is it after all? Identification paralyzes the listener's effectiveness in the caring relationship. In the extreme, the listener is overcome by the situation and the focus shifts from the needs of the care receiver to those of the caring minister.

❧

Imagine yourself in a hospital emergency room following an accident in which your leg has been badly injured and is bleeding profusely. Here are some of the reactions of the staff:

NURSE: "Oh, I've seen much worse."

DOCTOR: "I've got to get out of here. Your wound reminds me of the time my husband broke his leg. You should have seen it. The bone was sticking out and there was blood all over the place. I think I'm going to be sick." *As the doctor rushes out, one of the nurses follows her out.*

I.V. NURSE: *The I.V. nurse begins to insert the needle into your hand. As you wince slightly he comments,* "Don't be such a baby. This will only hurt for a moment."

DOCTOR: *A second doctor arrives to replace the first (who fainted in the hallway). With a big smile on his face he gives you the reassuring news:* "Cheer up! When this is all over, you'll still have one good leg left."

This bizarre scene was painted to exaggerate reactions that are not helpful to the healing process. Yet, to a lesser degree, they are the common responses we hear every day:

"Think of others who are much worse off."

"Tell me about it! When I had my gall bladder surgery, the doctor said it was the worse he'd ever seen."

"Come on, it can't be that bad."

"Thank God, you still have two children left."

"Cheer up, tomorrow is another day."

What are some of your pet-peeve reactions?

The skilled caring minister weds competency with compassion, detachment with support, discretion with comfort.

Spiritual Attentiveness

Pastoral caregivers who recognize their role as instruments and participants in God's grace discover that they are able both to give and receive spiritual energy. The pastoral relationship is one in which the listener stands in awe of God's activity in the life of the other person. Remember the job description. It can be summed up in the word "humility." The word, of course, does not mean that one is exalted as the superhero who swoops in to save the day. But neither does it signify an equally self-centered stance of denigrating one's gifts, skills, and call to participate in the healing process.

Spiritual attentiveness also involves our disposition to prayer, not simply "saying prayers" during the pastoral visit (dealt with in a later chapter), but carrying out the visit in an attitude of prayer. You are inviting God to be present in a very real way and even imagining that you and your care receiver are *both* listening to the movement of the Holy Spirit in your dialogue. The caring minister will also be strengthened by committing the pastoral relationship to prayer on a regular basis.

Throughout this book you will be encouraged to attend to your own spiritual growth through prayer, Scripture reflection, and other reading. Rather than being provided with a list of resources, *you* become the resource. Genuine caring ministry training prepares us from the inside out to become men and women of faith.

Conclusion

Another aspect of our practice in listening will be to spend a few minutes after each pastoral visit recalling the dialogue. Act as your own fair witness as you reflect upon the following questions:

- How attentive was I?

- What internal and external distractions kept me from listening?

- Did I allow the focus to shift to me?

- Was I forming in my mind what I would say before the person speaking was finished?

- What feelings did my care receiver express?

- What feelings do I now identify in myself?

- *Who did most of the talking?*

As you go about your week, begin to notice how you and others around you listen. Practice at the grocery store, in the office, with your family. Perhaps you will even encounter one of these persons:

- The elderly woman with vacant eyes sits in her wheelchair in the hallway of a nursing care center, her head hanging slightly. Her heart and mind are full of locked away memories and wisdom; there is no one left to listen.

- The widow whose husband died three months ago has given up the attempt to tell her friends about the loneliness that sweeps over her in the middle of the night. When she tried to explain to her best friend how the initial shock has turned into aching grief, her friend responded, "It will take time. Just remember Hal is in a better place." No one will really listen.

- The young unemployed husband and father finds himself sick with paralyzing fears and anxieties. Who will listen?

- The homeless transient wanders into the shelter requesting the use of a telephone book. He has lost track of all his family, but be thinks his sister might live in this city. Will the volunteer take a few minutes to listen?

How can you become a better listener?

Spiritual Application

Now in Jerusalem by the Sheep Gate there is a pool, called in Hebrew Beth-zatha, which has five porticoes. In these lay many invalids — blind, lame, and paralyzed. One man was there who had been ill for thirty-eight years. When Jesus saw him lying there and knew that he had been there a long time, he said to him, "Do you want to be made well?" The sick man answered him, "Sir, I have no one to put me into the pool when the water is stirred up; and while I am making my way, someone else steps down ahead of me." At once the man was made well, and he took up his mat and began to walk. (John 5:2–9)

Wasn't Jesus asking the obvious to the invalid: "Do you want to be made well?" The Scripture reveals that Jesus already knew he had been there a long time. Why then did he ask? I can think of several reasons why Jesus posed a question to the man before his healing:

- Jesus refrained from allowing his own good intentions to justify imposing himself upon another. There is no record of unsolicited healings; Jesus demonstrated the deepest respect for people.

- The invalid may have needed to verbalize his own desires and bring them into sharp focus for himself. Jesus knew the man needed healing, but he could not assume he wanted it. He may well have been one of those persons who "enjoyed" poor health. His sad state of affairs may have formed his identity and provided him with sympathy. It may have even been his means of making a living as a beggar. Jesus' gentle confrontation enabled him to hear and to voice his own longing.

- From what we know in the Gospels, Jesus conversed with people he healed. He didn't dispense miracles like so much cheap fast food. He entered into an unhurried dialogue with this man as he listened to his sad tale of disappointed hopes. Jesus loved to listen to people. He became distressed when a woman came up behind him and touched the hem of his garment. Perhaps he wheeled around because he had been denied the opportunity to hear her story and meet her face to face (Mark 5:25–34). These and other treasured stories reveal Jesus' sound pastoral style and his own unique gift of listening.

Loving God, in the name of Jesus in whose image we seek to grow, give us the humility, grace, and disposition to listen as he did. Amen.

❧ Chapter 4

Focus on Feelings – Part 1

*As God's chosen ones, holy and beloved, clothe yourselves with
compassion, kindness, humility, meekness, and patience. Bear with
one another and … above all, clothe yourselves with love, which
binds everything together in perfect harmony.* (Col. 3:12–14)

We continue to build on the gift and skill of listening in each caring ministry chapter. As previously mentioned, listening is a gift of
the caregiver's full attention to *all of the information,* the *whole
story,* and to the *feelings* of the care receiver. The expression of
feelings is one of the primary ways in which trust is nurtured and
relationship is deepened with the care receiver. The purpose of this
chapter is (1) to develop a sensitivity to the feeling world of the care
receiver; (2) to learn how to acknowledge, honor, and invite communication of feelings; and (3) to move from the functional level
(what people *do*) to the deeper level of how a person uniquely relates, responds, and reacts to the situation (who a person *is,* the
unique self).

Consider the following true story as an illustration of the need for
the communication of feelings:

The priest arrived at the nursing home to pay a pastoral call
to an elderly man just recently admitted. He was wheelchair-
bound and nearly blind. For the past year his frail wife had
undertaken to care for him at home, but the demands had taken
their toll on her, both physically and emotionally. After she herself collapsed and was hospitalized, the decision was reached
to place him in a nursing care center. As the priest entered
the room the following conversation was taking place between
husband and wife:

MR. KLONDIKE: "I want to go home. Take me home today."

MRS. KLONDIKE: "Honey, you know I can't do that. I can't take care of you."

MR. KLONDIKE: "We'll hire someone to take care of me. Get me out. You don't care about me."

MRS. KLONDIKE: "But we can't afford it, and you know I've been sick."

MR. KLONDIKE: "This is a terrible place."

MRS. KLONDIKE: "Oh, no, this is a wonderful facility. They'll take good care of you."

MR. KLONDIKE: "No it isn't. They are stealing from me already. I hate it here."

MRS. KLONDIKE: "Now you know that isn't true. The staff are carefully screened."

MR. KLONDIKE: "No, they are not. One of the nurse's aides hit me."

Mr. Klondike feels helpless. He has lost control of his own choices. Very angry and frustrated, he expresses his feelings by making demands. Mrs. Klondike mistakenly thinks that stating the facts of the situation will calm him down. Instead of calming him down, this provokes more anger, resulting in more unrealistic demands.

Not only did Mr. Klondike's voice become louder and louder, he also began to push his wheelchair back and forth until by the end of the fruitless conversation, he was banging into the bed, the night stand, and nearly into his wife. The priest wisely decided not to give frail Mrs. Klondike an on-the-spot lesson in listening to feelings. Instead, she attempted to support each one by affirming how sad and difficult the situation had become. She later spent time with each one separately, simply listening to the outpouring of feelings expressed by both husband and wife. Let us examine what went awry in this episode.

- Mrs. Klondike offers more facts: "We can't afford it."

- Mr. Klondike's frustration escalates to the point of fabricating an incident of stealing to get her attention.

- Mrs. Klondike argues the point and even includes a "cheer up" statement: "This is a wonderful facility. They'll take good care of you."

- This only leads to a further escalation of Mr. Klondike's anger. In desperation he fabricates yet another, more serious accusation. His anger and frustration are finally acted out as he exerts his last vestige of control by banging his wheelchair into furniture and gesturing toward her.

What Mr. Klondike needed most was the acknowledgment of his feelings. That alone could have served to help deescalate his mounting frustration. How different the conversation might have been if Mrs. Klondike had been able to offer alternative responses such as:

"Yes, I know you're unhappy (sad, angry, etc.)"

"This is a difficult time for you."

"I'm so sad we had to do this."

Note that Mrs. Klondike was well-meaning in her responses. However, she was operating under the mistaken idea that we can talk people out of the way they feel. We cannot fault Mrs. Klondike. She had her own overwhelming problems plus the added guilt of making the final decision to do what she saw was best for her husband. Her own physical weakness and closeness to the situation made it unrealistic to expect her to fill the role of skilled listener. This is a perfect example of how the caring minister can be a source of healing. The pastoral caregiver contributes the paradoxical ability to be both detached and compassionate. The caring minister is able to listen to feelings when family members or others cannot through no fault of their own. In the case of Mr. and Mrs. Klondike, each one needed a supportive companion to invite the sharing of feelings without judgment, without the need to change feelings, and without the compulsion of needing to solve a problem.

Definition of Feelings

Feelings are emotional responses to our internal and external world. They provide us with a means of communicating our experience. Our feelings surface through words as well as actions.

The following partial list demonstrates just some of the diverse feelings projected through actions. Do not be too quick to identify a feeling from an action alone. Both joy and despair are feelings that can be expressed by crying.

Action	Feelings Indicated
Laughter	Joy, happiness, pleasure, amusement, nervousness
Crying	Grief, anger, bitterness, hurt, sadness, embarrassment, joy, fear, despair, amusement
Sighing	Apathy, boredom, fatigue, relaxation, contentedness, listlessness
Yawning	Boredom, tiredness, relaxation, contentedness, listlessness
Yelling or Raised Voice	Enthusiasm, anger, excitement, fear, astonishment, elation, fury, joy, shock, surprise

Notice that all feelings do not carry the same degree of intensity. Annoyance is no less a feeling than anger. Amusement is no less a feeling than jubilation, but simply is less intense. We use the entire range of emotions to form our richly textured interactive ability.

Keep in mind the following points regarding feelings:

- Feelings alert us to what is important, in rating them, as it were, on a scale from 1 to 10. A 10 will require more attention and energy than a 2.

- It is healthy both to "edit" feelings and to give them expression. The situation and the level of intensity enable us to choose where, when, how, and with whom we share our feelings.

- Feelings are there and real even when we lack the capacity to surface and name them.

- Feelings are unique to each individual. Two people may react quite differently to the same circumstances.

- We are each responsible for our own feelings. No one can *make* us feel as we do, for example, "You infuriated me when you came home an hour late for dinner." Such a response presumes intention, fails to consider circumstances, and surrenders control over one's feelings to someone else. Alternative responsible statements might have been: "I felt angrier and angrier with each passing moment," or "I didn't know whether I should be angry or frightened."

- Feelings are neither good nor bad in themselves. Sadness or anger are not "bad" emotions in and of themselves. Any emotion can be used either appropriately or inappropriately.

We can allow feelings to control us or to serve us. They serve us best when we are able to acknowledge, honor, and appropriately communicate them with ourselves and others.

The Caring Minister's Role

Most of us were taught as youngsters that we ought not to express certain emotions. Anger was at the top of the list, especially for "good Christians." The attempt was made to screen out the feeling of anger from our emotional experience. But as we read the Scriptures, we will notice that the emotion of anger is reported. It has not been edited out of the record of God's activity with humanity. We discover throughout the Bible many episodes of anger. God reportedly was angry with Moses, Aaron, David, and all of Israel, just to name a few instances. David was angry with God, as was Jonah, who was "angry enough to die" (Jon. 4:9). Our Judeo-Christian history does not screen out, deny, or cover up the events, experiences, or consequences of anger. Perhaps one of the best statements regarding anger, for our purposes, is from Ephesians 4:25–26:

> So then, putting away falsehood, let all of us speak the truth to our neighbors, for we are members of one another. Be angry but do not sin; do not let the sun go down on your anger.

This passage invites us to be truthful with each other about relationships. It acknowledges and honors anger but also cautions against allowing anger to be acted out destructively. There is encouragement to deal with anger before the "sun goes down," which does not imply that anger should be denied, repressed, suppressed, or buried.

Anger provides a good working example of an emotion that can cause discomfort when expressed. The more we understand it as a part of our experience, the better we will be able to minister to those who carry unacknowledged and silent anger. The caring minister becomes instrumental in assisting the care receiver to deal with emotions through the gentle art of acknowledging, honoring, and inviting communication of feelings.

Acknowledging Feelings

Have you ever felt agitated but didn't know why? As you reviewed the events of the day, you recalled an incident in which you felt hurt by a remark made by a co-worker. As you recognized your own reaction of hurt, the feeling suddenly left you. Perhaps, on reflection, you realized the person did not intend to hurt you or you determined that on a scale of 1 to 10, it was a 1 and required no more of your energy. You may have reached the conclusion that the remark was indeed intentional and that you would deal with it on that basis. Whatever the options, you noticed that once you surfaced the feeling for what it was, you were able to let go of its power to keep you in an agitated state. Often the simple act of acknowledging a feeling is all one needs in order to let it go.

The caring ministry relationship creates the forum and opportunity to surface and acknowledge feelings. Supportive listening is the key. Since most of us have been conditioned to steer away from certain emotions, it will be necessary to be alert to tendencies that impede the process, for example:

Making Judgments	"How could you feel that way under those circumstances?"
Devaluing	"You shouldn't feel that way."
Protecting	"Don't cry."
Diverting	"So, how was the rest of your day?"

Using clichés	"The rain falls on the just and the unjust."
	"She's in a better place."
Labeling	CARE RECEIVER: "I felt agitated at the bus driver."
	CARING MINISTER: "Oh, so you felt really hostile." (*Agitated to hostile is a big jump.*)
Generalizing	CARE RECEIVER: "I felt so sad when I saw the homeless woman."
	CARING MINISTER (*thinks to herself*): "She is one depressed lady." (*The sadness was situational; depression is a complex of emotions.*)

Never, never say, "You shouldn't feel that way," even with the best intentions. Simply recognize how a person does feel. Respect the uniqueness of that experience and allow that person to express it.

Honoring Feelings

After feelings have been recognized ("Yes, I can tell you're hurt"), the caring minister takes the next step by honoring and accepting the feeling ("I can see how you could be hurt in that situation"). By honoring the feelings of the care receiver, the caregiver is in effect affirming, "I accept the way you feel in your circumstances." Caregivers need to exert caution with regard to assigning their own reactions to the care receiver. Guard against evaluating the feelings on the basis of how you would have reacted. We can honor someone else's feelings *even when we do not agree with that person.*

CARE RECEIVER: "I hate all Arabs. The only good Arab is a dead Arab."

CARING MINISTER: "That's a pretty strong feeling." (*recognition and acceptance*)

CARE RECEIVER: "Yes, I'm so scared for our soldier boys over there and here I am a little old lady unable to do anything."

CARING MINISTER: "You're feeling frightened, helpless?"

CARE RECEIVER: "Yes, I can't do anything, but I do pray for them."

CARING MINISTER: "Tell me how you pray."

CARE RECEIVER: "I ask God to protect our boys and to wipe the Arabs off the face of the earth."

CARING MINISTER: "You've expressed some pretty strong feelings to me: hate, concern, fear, helplessness. What would it be like if you were to pray those feelings to God?"

CARE RECEIVER: "Oh, I never thought of that. It might be helpful."

The caring minister did not feel the same hatred or agree that obliteration would be an appropriate response. Notice how he was able to honor and unearth the deep emotions that fueled the woman's hatred. Note, also, that the woman never even sought agreement.

Inviting Communication of Feelings

In the above example, the caring minister acknowledged, honored, and also invited further communication of those feelings by asking a question ("You're feeling frightened, helpless?") and also by reflecting her feelings back to her (scared = frightened; unable to do anything = helpless). The dialogue gave her the freedom to describe her feelings and even gave her the opportunity to choose to express them to God. At the beginning of the dialogue a statement from the caring minister such as, "God wants us to love our enemies," would probably have prevented the expression of further emotions and would not have contributed to the building of trust between the two.

The level of self-disclosure and expression of feelings is entirely the decision of the care receiver. Although the role of the caregiver is to allow those feelings to surface and to provide an atmosphere of trust and safety, it is *never* to force the expression of feelings. Some emotions are too overwhelming to handle all at once. Be sensitive to your care receiver's fragility and respect his or her individual needs and comfort zone.

Conclusion

You have already been exposed to the practice of reflective listening in some of the examples used. It is vital for caregivers, and it requires some practice. In the next chapter, reflective listening will be discussed in greater depth.

Spiritual Application

The importance of shared feelings and the building of trust in the caring ministry relationship is like that found in the relationship between spiritual director and directee. The spiritual director functions as a catalyst only and is careful not to get in the way of God's self-disclosure. The spiritual director's primary role is to call the directee back to the encounter with God, especially in matters of spiritual discernment. People often treat discernment and spiritual direction as separate projects, focusing on the end result and searching for a sign or answer outside of themselves. As people share their struggle to discern God's guidance regarding a particular decision, a wise spiritual director will pose the following reflective questions:

1. What is your relationship with God at this time?

2. How are you cultivating the relationship?

3. When you dialogue with God about this question of discernment, do you express your feelings about it?

Interestingly enough, the answer to no. 3 is usually "no." As the dialogue is explored, it becomes clear that the prayer has centered on facts and results rather than feelings. God is treated like an efficient secretary instead of an intimate friend. True discernment is a natural outgrowth of a rich relationship with God. It comes about more by listening to and trusting the Holy Spirit from within than by experiencing direct unusual signs from without (although such signs may confirm what's happening within).

A woman who had been in spiritual direction for years came to me one day in a state of confusion and turmoil. She had just finished a degree and had many questions about vocation and call. She was seeking answers to these hard questions, but God seemed to be silent on the subject. "Tell me about your relationship with God," I said. The next few minutes revealed that her once rich and intimate rapport with God had turned dry and lifeless. As she experienced aridity in prayer, she began to abandon her daily practices of prayer and reading. How could she even hear God if God was to give her a word of guidance? Since she had been faithful and intentional about her spiritual life, she was able to grasp the connection immediately between her lack of discernment and her lapse in prayer. We never did talk about the hows and wherefores of her next career move. Instead we reflected on her feelings and on the reclaiming of communication with her true source of life. Within a few weeks her path of vocation unfolded almost effortlessly as she got in touch with the treasure hidden within her heart.

In a similar fashion, the caring minister focuses on the areas that will build a trusting relationship rather than on problem solving. Not only is this relationship cultivated with the care receiver, but also with God, who initiates healing and hope.

Chapter 5

Focus on Feelings – Part 2

"By this everyone will know that you are my disciples, if you have love for one another."   (John 13:35)

Just for today, Lord, let me set down my fear of not knowing and extend myself to the growth of another. Where there is strife, let me sow love, not facts. Where there is grief, let me sow comfort, not capability. Where there is need, let me extend my hand to help, and not merely point the way. Amen.*

The previous chapter outlined the importance of feelings in the healing process. The expression of feelings invites the development of a trusting relationship between caring minister and care receiver. It will be worthwhile to review these basics from time to time, particularly at the beginning of a ministry assignment.

- Feelings are the emotional responses to the internal and external world of a person.

- Feelings provide means and ways of communicating emotional responses.

- People use the entire range of emotions to form the human interactive ability.

- Feelings are real even when a person is unable to access them.

- Feelings are unique to each individual and can reveal a person's inner depths.

---

*Prayer by Marian Yagel McBay from *The Upper Room Disciplines 1991*. Copyright © 1990 by The Upper Room. Used by permission of Upper Room Books. All rights reserved.

- Each of us is ultimately responsible for our own feeling responses.

- The caring minister can be most effective by acknowledging, honoring, and inviting communication of feelings and avoiding the practices of judging, devaluing, protecting, diverting, using clichés, labeling, diminishing, or forcing the expression of feelings.

- The caring minister needs to be sensitive to the care receiver's needs, fragility, and comfort zone, respecting the care receivers unique capacity and desire for self-disclosure and practicing gentle attentiveness to the slow unfolding of the Holy Spirit's action.

This chapter continues the discussion of feelings with a special emphasis on reflective listening and the self-disclosure of the caring minister.

Reflective Listening

One of the most valuable tools of the good listener is the ability to reflect back to the care receiver the feelings that person is experiencing. Skillful reflective listening indicates that the caring minister is paying attention and is beginning to understand the care receiver's experience. Reflective listening can also help those in pain listen to themselves in a new way and to identify deep, unrecognized thoughts and feelings.

There are many ways to practice reflective listening, the simplest of which is repeating back, verbatim, what was stated. This may sound contrived or too simple, but it can be dramatic in its effectiveness as illustrated in this true story.

A caring minister was attending one of the Ladies' Guild meetings and approached one of the older members, who had been absent for some time. Annie, the older woman, had taken care of her handicapped daughter, Mary, for fifty-five years. Recently, Annie suffered a stroke, and her other children placed Mary in a group home, where she seemed to be very happy.

CARING MINISTER: "Annie, how are you? I haven't seen you for ages!"

ANNIE: "Oh, I've had a stroke, and when I was in the hospital, my son and daughter put Mary in an apartment building for handicapped people." *Annie begins to cry.* "They say I can't take care of her anymore. She's been with me all of her life. I've always taken care of her but they say she's better off where she is. But she's my baby!"

CARING MINISTER: *Places her hand gently on Annie's hand, looks her in the eye, and replies,* "Yes, she's your baby."

ANNIE: *Looks up a little stunned,* "Oh thank you. You understand."

Later, when the meeting ends, the caring minister bids Annie goodbye. Annie takes her hand and says, "Thank you again. You've helped me so much."

Notice that the caring minister did not even need to name the feelings Annie was expressing. By repeating her very words with the same inflections, the caring minister let Annie know she had been heard, and her feelings were being acknowledged and honored. Annie did not need one more person in her life to set her straight on the facts. She knew well the reality of the situation. All she needed was for someone to recognize that she felt as if she had "lost her baby." Annie expressed several other emotions in this episode. Think about what she revealed in her responses.

Reflecting back can also take the form of repeating just a portion of the statement:

CARE RECEIVER: "I was so hurt when I found out I wasn't invited to the party."

CARING MINISTER: "You felt really hurt."

It can also be done by restating in one's own words what was said:

CARE RECEIVER: "I'm so mad at the doctor. I gave up smoking and I'm still sick!"

CARING MINISTER: "You're really angry!"

CARE RECEIVER: "Yes, I'm really angry!"

By restating the feeling with slightly different words, it also invites clarification from the care receiver:

CARING MINISTER: "You're really angry!"

CARE RECEIVER: "Well, I guess I'm really more disappointed than angry."

CARING MINISTER: "Can you tell me a little more about that?"

We can also exercise reflective listening by observing the physical behaviors of the care receiver *without drawing conclusions.*

CARING MINISTER (*after several visits*): "I notice you've smiled several times today. It's the first time since we've been meeting I've seen you smile."

CARE RECEIVER: "Really? I guess I'm not as depressed as I was."

The gentle restating of the care receiver's words serves as a check on the caring minister against forming premature opinions or rushing the process of sharing. Reflective listening provides time and space to allow the feelings to simmer and surface. It gives both persons the opportunity to notice the important feelings and determine which are worthy of further exploration.

Self-Disclosure of the Caring Minister

The role of a pastoral caregiver is both detached and compassionate at the same time. Healthy detachment prevents the caregiver from becoming paralyzed or overwhelmed by the feelings or experience of the one in crisis. However, detachment is not practiced at the expense of compassion and permits the caregiver to become a true source of strength and healing.

Of course the caring minister cannot help being touched by another's grief or pain. The wise and judicious self-disclosure of the caregiver can, at times, be beneficial in surfacing the feelings of the care receiver. In sharing personal feelings and information, the caring minister may find the following guidelines useful:

- **Try to avoid lengthy stories that make it difficult for the other to continue.**

CARE RECEIVER: "My dad was in a coma for two days before he died."

CARING MINISTER: "So was my mom. I'll never forget how the family all gathered around her and said their goodbyes. You know, the hearing is the last thing to go, so it's important to speak to the person in a coma. That was a special time for our family, and we were really supported by the hospital staff. One nurse even cried with us at the bedside..." *and on and on.....*

The caring minister has a fine story to tell, but this is not the appropriate time or place. The care receiver has been cut off and it would be awkward to resume the story.

- **If it seems appropriate to share a feeling or an experience, make certain it contributes to the healing process of the care receiver.**

CARE RECEIVER: "Since I took care of my husband for so many years, people expected me to be relieved that he died, but I'm not."

CARING MINISTER: "I think I know what you mean. When my dad died after a similar illness, people said it was a blessing. All I knew was that I missed him. Is that sort of what you mean?"

CARE RECEIVER: "Oh, yes, you really understand. I loved taking care of him. He was my husband and I loved him and I miss him."

In this example, the caring minister shared briefly and used the sharing to focus back on the other's experience.

- **When appropriate, share your personal feelings about what the care receiver is enduring.** For example:

"That's so sad."

"I think I would have felt angry too."

"It hurts me to hear how your husband treats you."

None of the above statements offers advice or calls for a solution.

The question is often asked, "Should the caring minister cry?" There are times when a pastor just cannot help it because the situation is so touching. Here are a few guideline questions for the pastoral caregiver:

- "Will my tears shift the focus to *my* pain and away from the care receiver's pain?"

- "Will my crying become so uncontrolled that I become the one who needs ministry?"

- "Whose needs are being met?"

- "Is it more appropriate in this instance to defer my tears to a time when I can be alone and process the true source of my feelings?"

If the caring minister can cry *with* a person and still keep the focus on the care receiver, it can be a time of sharing sorrow in a very caring way.

Many pastoral caregivers have learned to do their grieving in private, in prayer, and with spiritual directors. This allows them to be free to minister more effectively and to be present as a "wounded healer" rather than the bleeding wounded.

It is natural that feelings, memories, reactions, and insights arise for the caring minister in the pastoral relationship. The appropriate place to share and process these stories and feelings is with the leader or facilitator or in a shared ministry support group. For the most part, it is inadvisable to share in-depth personal experiences with the care receiver. This could reverse the roles or cause the care receiver to develop a sense of guilt and responsibility for the caring minister's reactions.

Conclusion

A wise therapist once said, "Feelings don't get buried dead. They get buried alive." Feelings do not go away simply by being ignored, repressed, suppressed, or denied. When deeply buried, feelings are adept at finding other modes of expression such as illness, coldness, or the slow erosion of communicative relationships. The caring minister offers yet another precious gift when gently inviting the sharing of feelings in a safe, supportive environment.

Spiritual Application

> *May those who sow in tears*
> *reap with shouts of joy.*
> *Those who go out weeping,*
> *bearing the seed for sowing,*
> *shall come home with shouts of joy,*
> *carrying their sheaves.*
> (Ps. 126:5–6)

We can learn much from the ancient people and how they handled their feelings and losses. This psalm was written to celebrate the Hebrew exiles' return from Babylonian captivity. So why the tears? They had made new lives in captivity; a foreign land had become familiar. It was a minority who chose to face another trek across the wilderness and reclaim Zion. The promise of a restored nation and rebuilt temple did not diminish the sacrifices and difficulties they had to face. They dealt honestly with the reality of leaving and did not idealize the tough journey ahead. Sowing in tears referred to the custom of ritual weeping as the seed was sown in the ground. It was believed that the tears had a magical quality to release the life buried deep within the seed. This redeeming quality of tears gives rise to an assurance of reaping with shouts of joy.

We might recall this psalm as we sit with those who need to weep. Their tears can water the dry soul thirsting for new directions. This psalm also reminds us that events of our own choosing and new paths of a positive nature are, nevertheless, occasions for some degree of grief.

On a worldwide scale we have witnessed newfound freedom as a cause for enormous grief and loss. The crumbling of the Berlin Wall and the break-up of the Soviet bloc turned people's lives upside down. As powers became realigned, people with guaranteed livelihoods found themselves on their own. For many, freedom was not all it was cracked up to be.

We may encounter individuals who are experiencing unexpected grief as they move through a positive transition. A woman leaving an abusive husband is faced with new responsibilities and financial challenges. Job promotions may require a move across the country and the loss of all that is familiar and comfortable. Death that follows a long-term illness is not simply regarded as "a blessing" by a grieving family, but as the loss of an irreplaceable loved one. Almost any change results in an internal shift that challenges a person to explore a new territory for living. The caring minister provides a safe place for expression and reflection.

Just for today, Lord, let me set down my fear of not knowing and extend myself to the growth of another. Where there is strife, let me sow love, not facts. Where there is grief, let me sow comfort, not capability. Where there is need, let me extend my hand to help, and not merely point the way. Amen. *

Chapter 6

Compatibility Checking

Do not be conformed to this world, but be transformed by the renewing of your minds, so that you may discern what is the will of God — what is good and acceptable and perfect.   (Rom. 12:2)

In learning to listen and in cultivating the ability to focus on feelings, we have received the most valuable and basic pastoral tools. The posture of listening is evidence of humble openness to God's activity in the interaction. It also creates an environment of growing trust. Focusing on feelings by acknowledging, honoring, and inviting communication allows the care receiver to get in touch with inner emotional responses. The expression of previously unexplored feelings can be a major factor in a person's healing process. Every pastoral ministry interaction will be supported by these two skills in one form or another.

We've discussed the uniqueness and individuality of each person's feeling world. Perceptions of events, crises, and situations are shaped by individual past history as well as physical and emotional make-up. This is supported by the evidence that several people can witness the same event or attend the same meeting and express entirely different perceptions, feelings, and assumptions. While each person owns a unique inner experience, it does not necessarily follow that it is entirely congruent or compatible with reality. The healthy person is always willing to check self-knowledge with world knowledge, interior insight with exterior data, private feelings with public behaviors. The adept pastoral caregiver helps the care receiver to make the vital connections between the inner and outer experience.

Think about a young teenage girl who suffers from anorexia nervosa. She is sixteen pounds underweight, yet when she views her image in the mirror, all she can perceive is a body that is grossly fat. She becomes obsessed with weight loss and exercise. Her distorted interior self-image is incongruent and incompatible with exterior reality. If carried to the extreme, this can lead to death. Telling her how skinny she appears or even attempting to set her straight on the facts ("You only weigh eighty-two pounds") does nothing to enable her to see the incongruent nature of her private self-revulsion and her true appearance and behaviors. Thankfully, there are highly specialized programs with experts who assist people with this disorder. They patiently lead the suffering individual (mostly young women) to a place where she can see her true image reflected in the mirror. When reality is finally faced, healing begins. Although dealing with this disorder is beyond the scope and training of the caring minister, anorexia is an excellent and extreme example of feelings and perceptions that are not compatible with visible behaviors and facts.

Testing Experience

Compatibility checking is a way in which the caring minister can assist the care receiver to test the *perception* of an experience against the actual experience. Do the inner feelings make sense when examined in the light of the outer experience (the who, what, when, where, how)? Compatibility checking builds upon the reflection and expression of feelings and takes them a step further by testing their usefulness to growth. Inner feelings and perceptions that are out of proportion or incompatible with the event may restrict the ability to change, to mend relationships, and to move forward while allowing the situation to become a learning experience.

Key elements in compatibility checking include the following:

- Compatibility checking should be used after a relationship of trust is established. It follows, and *never replaces,* listening and focusing on feelings.

- Compatibility checking should not be practiced in an interrogative style or in a tone of voice that may come across as doubtful, judgmental, or adversarial.

- The focus remains on the care receiver's perceptions, *not* on those of the pastoral caregiver.

- The effective use of compatibility checking will lovingly assist the care receiver to face possible incongruities that have created obstacles to further growth, freedom, and healing.

- Compatibility checks are appropriate when the care receiver appears to be assigning motives to others, which may or may not be valid, and when the care receiver makes broad depreciative generalizations, for example:

"Jim in the office is out to get me." (assumes motive)

"I'm a failure." (depreciative generalization)

"She's insecure." (depreciative generalization)

"He *always* disagrees with me." (depreciative generalization)

How to Use Compatibility Checks

Quite simply, checking compatibility uses the basic journalistic questions of *who, what, when, where,* and *how.* These questions can reveal to the care receiver inconsistencies in perceptions and areas where denial or depreciative feelings have unnecessarily added to the pain. The caring minister does not deny or judge the feelings but allows the person to assess their usefulness as premises to potential healing.

Compatibility checking moves from the *general* to the *specific:*

CARE RECEIVER: "Everyone thinks he's a liar."

CARING MINISTER: "*Who* exactly thinks (or has said) he is a liar?"

—

CARE RECEIVER: "She *always* insults me."

CARING MINISTER: "Can you share with me what she has said?"

—

CARE RECEIVER: "He never supports me."

CARING MINISTER: "Can you be a little more specific?"

—

CARE RECEIVER: "I didn't get the job because the young woman interviewing me thought I was too old."

CARING MINISTER: "Did she indicate that your age was a factor?"

CARE RECEIVER: "No, but she was so young and attractive I knew she thought I was over the hill."

CARING MINISTER: "What did she say that led you to this conclusion?"

CARE RECEIVER: "She didn't say anything."

CARING MINISTER: "How do you feel about your age and your looks?"

Words such as "always," "never," "everyone," and "no one" should alert the caregiver to the need to move into specifics.

⚬⚬⚬

Use the following approach when the person is forfeiting control over feelings and choices:

CARE RECEIVER: "He makes me drink too much." *RET*

CARING MINISTER: "How can he make you drink too much?"

—

CARE RECEIVER: "I'll have to support my brother after Mom dies."

CARING MINISTER: "Who made that decision?"

CARE RECEIVER: "Mom has been supporting him and she will expect me to do the same."

CARING MINISTER: "Has she discussed this with you?" *or* "Do you wish to support him?" *or* "Are you financially able to support him?"

CARE RECEIVER: "No."

CARING MINISTER: "What might be some of the options?"

The discerning caring minister will not fall into the trap of making suggestions, which would probably be answered with "Yes, but...." Instead, the caring minister offers the person an opportunity to think about his or her own choices and alternatives. This process should come across without appearing blatantly confrontational, with discernment again the guiding factor.

Observe this conversation between a very bright, attractive woman and a caring minister:

CARE RECEIVER: "I'm so ugly and unappealing."

CARING MINISTER: "What exactly about your appearance is ugly or unappealing?" (*Note: the minister does not say, "You're not ugly."*)

CARE RECEIVER: "I must have lost my looks. My husband had an affair with another woman."

This woman's inner feeling of being ugly is deeply rooted in hurt, betrayal, and rejection. As the caring minister took the time to check the compatibility of the inner perception with the actual reality (she *is* pretty), the woman found she had no specific information to support the statement (for instance, "My nose is too big"). However, she revealed deeper feelings prompted by her husband's infidelity. It may seem kind and polite to have said, "Oh, no, you're not ugly; you're very stunning." But such a statement would result in the following:

- It would cut off the care receiver's ability to see for herself the incongruity between her statement and reality.

- It would shift dialogue from the care receiver's perceptions to those of the caring minister.

- It would conveys a desire to conclude the dialogue: "No, you're pretty and that's that."

Compatibility checks keep the focus on the inner and outer world of the care receiver. This is not to indicate that a caregiver cannot express feelings, but the caregiver conveys feelings without imposing them on the other, for example:

> CARING MINISTER: "I'm having difficulty connecting his behavior with your reaction. Can you help me with that?" *or* "I'm feeling confused about ..." *or* "I think I missed something when you said ..."

Statements along these lines invite the care receiver to explore further the threads that tie together the inner and outer worlds. In the collaboration and interchange between these two worlds the interior world provides depth while the exterior world sheds light upon the inner workings of the psyche and spirit.

You may have noticed that "why?" is not included as a useful question in compatibility checking. "Why" leaves the way open for generalizations, interpretations, and subjective judgments.

> CARE RECEIVER: "She's trying to make me look bad at work."

> CARING MINISTER: "Why?"

> CARE RECEIVER: "Because she's jealous of me."

> CARING MINISTER: "Why is she jealous of you?"

> CARE RECEIVER: "I'm sure it's because I have more education."

In the above example, no data has been given to support the assumption of jealousy. The caring minister can assist in the process with concrete questions:

> CARING MINISTER: "What things has she done that make you look bad?"

> CARE RECEIVER: "I don't know, but everybody thinks so."

> CARING MINISTER: "Who exactly has said this?"

Or another example:

> CARE RECEIVER: "I called Jim and told him what I thought."

> CARING MINISTER: "Why did you do that?"

This sounds as if the caring minister thinks it was a bad choice. A better response would be:

CARING MINISTER: "What did you tell him?"

When a woman filed for divorce from an alcoholic husband, she shared with her caring minister the difficulty she was having in living in the same house with her husband until the divorce was final. The caring minister asked, "What is preventing you from selling your house?" The woman looked somewhat startled and suddenly the picture became clear. What seemed obvious to the caring minister had not occurred to her because of her personal pain and injured self-esteem. The couple quickly sold the house, and she no longer had to be subjected to the awkward, unpleasant home situation.

Asking concrete questions works well even with the confused, the disoriented, and those struggling with forms of senile dementia.

CARE RECEIVER: "They made me sleep outside last night."

CARING MINISTER: "Why would anyone want to do that?"

This translates as "I think you made it up, and I don't believe you." Better responses would be:

CARING MINISTER: "Where did you sleep outside?" or "Did you sleep in a bed?" or "Who made you sleep outside?"

These concrete questions affirm: "I take you seriously. I am interested in what you are saying." In most cases this will deflate the fantasy and draw the person into the present moment. Such fantasies can also be used to explore feelings that are being expressed through metaphors.

CARE RECEIVER: "They made me sleep outside last night."

CARING MINISTER: "Are you feeling left out or pushed out?"

CARE RECEIVER: "Yes, I don't know where I am supposed to be."

CARING MINISTER: "You're feeling confused about where to go?"

CARE RECEIVER: "I can't remember where my room is."

CARING MINISTER: "That's sad. It's hard when you can't remember."

CARE RECEIVER: "Yes, I'm sad."

CARING MINISTER: "I'll help you find your room today if you wish."

CARE RECEIVER: "Yes, let's find my room."

The caring minister cannot cure the dementia but can treat this gentleman with respect and can build trust and rapport even if it is just for a day.*

Myers-Briggs Type Indicator

Those familiar with Myers-Briggs typology may have noticed that chapter 3, "The Gift of Listening," and chapters 4 and 5, "Focus on Feelings" are designed to help people get in touch with their inner world of intuitions and feelings. Compatibility checks complete the movement toward wholeness by allowing the interior and exterior realms to inform and give life to one another. The M.B.T.I. is a useful example of a healthy approach toward the compatibility of personality.

With the great contribution and insight of the M.B.T.I. (Myers-Briggs Type Indicator), we have discovered a system of human understanding that, when used correctly, encourages an *appreciative* attitude toward preferences and differences in both self and others. An appreciative use of the M.B.T.I. is characterized by the following:

- It allows for no wrong answers and no negative types.

- It allows us to understand our own unique disposition. For example:

---

*For further reading on compassionate listening with confused elderly people, refer to the outstanding work and research of Naomi Feil, A.C.S.W., as explained in *The Validation Breakthrough* (Baltimore: Health Professions Press, 1993).

"Ah ha! Now I know why I feel so depleted when I attend an all day conference."

"Oh, so that's why I feel so energized when I teach."

An extreme introvert may now claim such a disposition as good, positive, and essential even though some societies tend to reward extroverted behavior.

- It encourages a person to develop the complementary opposite typology, for example, an extrovert is challenged to nurture an interior life of depth or a sensate person might learn to listen and value the intuitive.

- It develops an appreciation for the preferences of others and increases understanding and acceptance of differences. For example:

  "Oh, now I know why my wife needs more time alone. She's not snubbing me. It's just the way she's made."

On the other hand, a depreciative use of M.B.T.I. is marked by the following:

- It makes generalized labels of self and others:

  "You introverts never want to have any fun."

  "I'm an intuitive. Don't confuse me with the facts."

- It is use as an excuse to avoid personal growth:

  "I'm an introvert, so I never go to group prayer meetings."

- It forms a quick analysis:

  "Oh, you're an E.N.F.P. I never get along with them."

  "You're a thinker and can't possibly know how I feel."

The intended use of the M.B.T.I. is to consider all types as viable and valuable. It defines each type with respect to its unique contribution and offers information about potential growing edges and complementary functions. All types are integral to the make-up of the world, and every person's gifts can add to the texture and character of a community.

Spiritual Application

When the wife of Uriah heard that her husband was dead, she made lamentation for him. When the mourning was over, David sent and brought her to his house, and she became his wife, and bore him a son.

But the thing that David had done displeased the Lord, and the Lord sent Nathan to David. He came to him, and said to him, "There were two men in a certain city, the one rich and the other poor. The rich man had very many flocks and herds; but the poor man had nothing but one little ewe lamb, which he had bought. He brought it up, and it grew up with him and with his children; it used to eat of his meager fare, and drink from his cup, and lie in his bosom, and it was like a daughter to him. Now there came a traveler to the rich man, and he was loath to take one of his own flock or herd to prepare for the wayfarer who had come to him, but he took the poor man's lamb, and prepared that for the guest who had come to him." Then David's anger was greatly kindled against the man. He said to Nathan, "As the Lord lives, the man who has done this deserves to die; he shall restore the lamb fourfold, because he did this thing, and because he had no pity."

Nathan said to David, "You are the man! Thus says the Lord, the God of Israel: I anointed you king over Israel, and I rescued you from the hand of Saul; I gave you your master's house, and you master's wives into your bosom, and gave you the house of Israel and of Judah; and if that had been too little, I would have added as much more. Why have you despised the word of the Lord, to do what is evil in his sight?"...David said to Nathan, "I have sinned against the Lord." Nathan said to David, "Now the Lord has put away your sin; you shall not die."

(2 Sam. 11:26–12:13)

- Identify David's areas of conflict and incompatibility.

- What strengths did Nathan possess to enable him to confront David?

- Reflect on the device he used to confront David. Why do you think it was successful?

- What is the result of his confrontation?

- Reflect on your own life. Have you ever been blessed with a Nathan?

Chapter 7

Understanding Loss, Grief, and Death – Part 1

"Come to me, all you that are weary and are carrying heavy burdens, and I will give you rest. Take my yoke upon you, and learn from me; for I am gentle and humble in heart, and you will find rest for your souls. For my yoke is easy, and my burden is light."
(Matt. 11:28–30)

∾∾∾

Lord, help me to see others through your eyes...to walk with them as you walk with me. Help me to let your light shine through me in my ministry as my help comes from only you, the source of all my comfort and courage. Be with me and let me speak your words to bring peace to those who are in pain. Amen.

Loss is a natural part of all life. It ebbs and flows as we move along our individual paths. We can walk with others and share their triumphs and their failures, be helpful and be helped, feel alone and yet know the loving support of others. Leaving the warmth of the womb and pushing into an unfriendly, cold world is our first knowledge of grief. As infants we endure a myriad of disturbances, from the seeming loss of our mother's attention, from breast to bottle to cup; we survive the many falls on the route to walking, sharing toys, and adapting to other people's demands through the difficult steps of growing up. Whether the loss of a favorite plaything or a pet; moving from a familiar house to an unknown neighborhood, a strange school, and a new grade; the death of a friend or a family member; a divorce, an unexplored relationship, or financial woes — each day losses are experienced by every one of us.

There are losses or deaths aside from dying. There is the death of a marriage (divorce); the death of a profession (firing, downsizing, retirement); the death of expected income (loss of job, physical or mental illness); the death of a child (beginning school, graduation, out of town move, unacceptable lifestyle, marriage); the death of one's health (chronic illness, amputation, loss of senses, that is, touch, taste, hearing, seeing, smell); the death of a familiar role.

In addition to the unpleasant experiences of our lives, there are positive events that may also be greeted with unexpected sadness. The basic law of physics "For every action there is a reaction" and the managerial maxim "Today's solutions create tomorrow's problems" may help to explain this. Consider a job promotion. There can be a change in relationships with old work friends should you become their supervisor. More money may mean more hours, more travel, a new set of acquaintances, another income bracket. Think of a newborn baby and the changes caused in the lives of parents. Everything is turned upside down from sleep, to work, to putting a new person's demands ahead of normal schedules. All through our lives when there are joyous celebrations there also seems to be a downside in which melancholy feelings emerge.

For any caring minister an understanding of the dynamics of grief and loss is a necessity. Acquainting ourselves with the reactions to loss, the stages of reorientation, and effective pastoral skills will help us to add competency to our caring.

Reactions to Loss

Webster's New World Dictionary defines grief as "an intense emotional suffering caused by loss, disaster or misfortune, acute sorrow, deep sadness." The initial responses of "intense emotional suffering" consist of shock, numbness, and disbelief.

Shock acts as a protection, for both body and psyche, against overwhelming trauma. It gives the person some time to take in the event in small bits. Shock helps the person to gradually summon the internal resources needed to cope.

Similar to shock, numbness is another defense against trauma. People are often paralyzed so that they cannot feel or do anything and are deprived of the power to move physically, spiritually, or emotionally.

The sense of unreality takes form in the refusal to believe. People reject the event as untrue and even fall into magical thinking: "If no one speaks of the death maybe it didn't occur."

Response of the Caring Minister

The caring role will be substantially the same as in any pastoral call requiring all the skills discussed in earlier chapters. However, for those called upon the scene at the earliest stage of crisis, some additional understanding is helpful.

The first reactions of shock, numbness, and disbelief are not only normal but also quite healthy, protecting the person from too many emotional stimuli all at once. We should be much more concerned for an individual who exhibits none of these symptoms and appears to take the crisis in stride. Knowing about these patterns helps alleviate fear for the caregiver.

The caregiver attends to this phase as a triage team might respond to a medical emergency. Since this first stage is also characterized by confusion, the pastoral minister can function as the one with the ability to establish an order for the assistance needed and to determine what is needed most in the present moment. At the scene of an accident injured parties suffering from shock are covered with blankets — a simple yet necessary act. The caregiver acts in the same way, providing small but necessary comforts at the time of crisis. Making necessary telephone calls or offering a glass of water (dehydration causes further confusion) fall into this category.

Caregivers can provide comfort with their presence even more than with words. This is the time to listen but not the time for examining feelings. That will come later when the shock wears off and the serious business of grief work begins. Listening and reflecting back what the person is expressing facilitates the needed emotional release and the movement away from denial.

We can offer encouragement with appropriate touch as we feel at ease to do so. Crisis is the time in life when people most feel the need to be embraced and touched. An embrace can be the blanket of reassurance to wrap around the newly hurt. In *The Anatomy of Bereavement* Beverly Raphael writes that "facial expressions of grief are like those of the distressed infant abandoned by its mother."* It is a natural reflex to respond to such pleas with hugs or touching the shoulders or clasping the hands. Many people have become nervous about the use of touch, but it would be cruel to abandon its use because of fearfulness. Touch is less advisable during the later stages of grief but is most appropriate at the initial crisis phase for those who feel at ease with it. For those who do not feel comfortable with touching other forms of empathic comfort can be employed, such as gentle words of reassurance and a quiet steady presence.

Do not attempt to argue a person into belief when that person is expressing disbelief. Practice the gentle art of reflecting back feelings while at the same time reviewing the loss:

CARING MINISTER: "Yes, it's so hard to believe Jeff is dead. It seems impossible that he was alive just an hour ago."

Disbelief will, on it own, give way to reality as the situation requires attention: forms need to be signed, telephone calls need to be made, and perhaps the body needs to be identified.

Intervene in any self-destructive behavior, but be considerate about interfering. A suitable intervention would be to question the wisdom of taking strong drugs to further numb the pain. Remind the care receiver that this will only delay the process. Inappropriate interference might be making funeral arrangements before the family has a chance to gather and compose their thoughts. In other words, stand by but don't smother; alleviate confusion but don't take over.

Clichés are seldom suitable, and in the case of sudden crisis they can even sting the already hurting soul. Avoid remarks such as: "It was a blessing... "; "God must have had a reason to take her... "; "It must have been God's will... "; "Something good will come of this... "; "It was meant to be... ". Even though there are times when death is a mercy or we trust that something good will rise out of the ashes, these comforting thoughts will unfold at a later time. In the crisis moment, however, such thoughts can act as a premature push to move the person too rapidly into reflection and away from

---

*Beverly Raphael, *The Anatomy of Bereavement* (New York: Basic Books, 1983), 353.

the reality of the present moment. At times the care receiver may use clichés to label the experience. Simply reflect back the statements, enabling the person to file them away for future use.

CARE RECEIVER: "I guess God has some reason for this tragedy."

CARING MINISTER: "You think some light might come out of this darkness?" (Don't argue theology.)

—

CARE RECEIVER: "Clare was sick for so long. I should be grateful she's not suffering anymore."

CARING MINISTER: "It's easy to feel sad and relieved at the same time" *or* "You're relieved she's not suffering anymore."

Pastoral Care during Grief Stages

Most lay pastoral care will take place after the time of crisis and the initial trauma is past. The short-term shock, numbness, and disbelief yield to the long-term enterprise of working through grief. Familiarity with these stages equips the caregiver with a sensitivity that well-meaning friends do not possess. Using the analogy of the triage and emergency medical response teams, in the initial phases of a crisis people are surrounded by caring friends, family, clergy, and professionals. It is following the trauma when support systems begin to be withdrawn that grieving people need a companion to accompany them on their healing journey. It can be compared to a long hospital stay after surgery. Personnel come and go and often do not spend much time, only making maintenance checks of blood pressure and temperature. The patient has much time alone to think and worry and speculate about the future but has few opportunities to express those concerns. Likewise the grieving person discovers a lonely path as people begin to withdraw after the funeral, the retirement party, the terminal diagnosis, the divorce, the accident, or the move to a nursing care facility. The church now has its best opportunity to be an intentional witness to the healing power of the faith community.

Blessed be the God of our Lord Jesus Christ, the God of mercies and the God of all consolations, who consoles in all our affliction, so that we may be able to console those who are in deep affliction with the consolation with which we ourselves are consoled by God. (2 Cor. 1:3–4)

People in pain are not isolated but part of a relationship that gives life. The power of the community is received from the very intimate communion of God, Father/Mother, Son, and Interactive Spirit. Caregiving is an extension and a tangible demonstration of our deeply valued covenant to love others as God loves us.

The responses to grieving, especially in the face of death, will be discussed in more detail in the next chapter. But before moving on, take some time to consider your own journeys of loss and draw upon your own experience as a resource for ministry. Recall a time of great loss in your life and review it prayerfully and contemplatively using the *lectio divina* method as a structure:

Read. Listen to your own story. Be present to the details and the information. Who was there? What was said and done? *Be silent for two minutes.*

Reflect. Now notice your own feelings and name each one. What gets your attention? What experience stands out to you? *Be silent for two minutes.*

Respond. Name any healing moments. Who helped you? What words brought consolation and what caused desolation? What were some of the things you did to support your own healing? Are you able to recall God's activity or grace-filled moments? Is there anything for which you can give thanks? *Be silent for two minutes.*

Rest. Offer up your story once more to God. Let go of the details, the feelings and responses. Release all to the Mystery, to the still point where God's action becomes hidden to our senses. *Be silent for two to twenty minutes.*

- Can you identify what others offered that was helpful and what was a hindrance?

- Did any new feelings surface that may have been long buried?

- Can you identify any areas that still need healing?
- What are the sacred elements of your story?
- How have you experienced being a beloved child of God?

Conclusion

We cannot walk the shoes of others, but we can bless them with our presence and our lack of fear. We understand others by first understanding ourselves. All of skills we have been talking about thus far play into our ministry with our care receiver. Listening, accepting and understanding feelings, compatibility checking, and intentional prayer, which reminds us to depend upon God our Helper, all combine to round out our gifts as a concerned confidant. Each one of us expresses our fears and, yes, our delights differently. However, all of us crave patience rather than pushing, peace rather than drama, and caring, trust, and respect so that we feel safe enough to share our griefs and our joys. It takes time to develop a dependable, confident climate in which experiences can be discussed and healing can take place.

Spiritual Application

In his book *Man's Search for Meaning*, Victor Frankl recounts the horror and triumph of being a concentration camp survivor. When liberation came, he and many other camp survivors had the same experience as they returned to their towns and villages. They longed to tell their stories and somehow work through their enormous pain and suffering. As they began to share their stories with people who had been their friends and neighbors before the war, they were stopped with the remark, "Oh, we know, we know, we've suffered too." They were cut off, and sadly they were left to deal with their trauma in private and in isolation.

It is human nature to avoid another's pain. It can bring up fears of our own that we might have to touch the places in our lives that are worn very thin by the rough handling of this world.

In the reading of the Passion, there is a great opportunity for us to get in touch with Jesus' pain. There is a terrible point in the narrative when the people shout, "Crucify him, Crucify him." I can hardly stand it, but somehow I must acknowledge that my sinfulness and my failure to love did contribute to his wounds.

Jesus, however, did not turn away from all that is painful in our human condition. He had every opportunity in the Garden of Gethsemane to say, "No, I will not touch their pain," but instead he chose to say no to his fears and yes to love. It was not that he believed so much in the value of suffering but that he believed in the power of love. Perhaps we cannot work through our own hurts until we are willing to get in touch with each other's. Jesus connected with the human race most intimately when he freely gave himself to the cross. In the darkness of his dying hour he affirmed light. Amid hatred he still trusted love. In desolation he experienced the consolation of the women who did not shy away from his suffering. In the face of helplessness they offered their presence. As death closed in upon them, all their love affirmed life.

Understanding Loss, Grief, and Death – Part 2

In all these things we are more than conquerors through him who loved us. For I am convinced that neither death, nor life, nor angels, nor rulers, nor things present, nor things to come, nor powers, nor height, nor depth, nor anything else in creation, will be able to separate us from the love of God in Christ Jesus.

(Rom. 8:37–39)

Loving God, we know death is not the conclusion of our lives but just the beginning of a new journey. We do not often handle this with grace and joy because of our human sadness at our losses. Help us trust in your love and your strength and be with us as we walk with others in their grief so that we can be more fully present to them. Let us be rich in the very real hope and knowledge that your love will never fail us. Amen.

The last chapter focused primarily on the reactions to sudden loss and our response as caring ministers. In this chapter we will examine ministry to those who are dying and to those who are left to grieve. Although the emphasis is on death and dying, the same dynamics and resources for healing can be applied to other types of bereavements.

The Journey of Death

One of the most valuable contributions in this field is that of Elisabeth Kübler-Ross. In her book *On Death and Dying* she identifies five steps one may go through after learning of a fatal illness:

Denial: disbelief and even refusal to face the reality of the situation

Anger: rage and frustration at the "unfairness" of life

Bargaining: contracting for an extension of time or a cure

Depression: natural reaction to the present or impending loss

Acceptance: a reordering of the time left — which can be a peaceful, sacred, holy time

In general, these steps seem to describe the framework in which people locate themselves when any loss, large or small, is endured. It is essential to understand that there is no fixed time frame nor rigid order for these steps. They are more like rungs on a ladder on which people move up and down as the grief process unfolds. Some people move through them rapidly only to find that anger or denial continue to resurface. Many dying persons never reach acceptance but continue to grasp at the hope of cure to the very end. Surprisingly, more than one stage can be visited at the same time.

In Psalm 22, David expresses abandonment, anger, comfort, loss, and victory all in one prayer:

> O my God, I cry by day, but you do not answer;
> and by night, but find no rest....
> Yet it was you who took me from the womb;
> you kept me safe on my mother's breast.
> (Ps. 22:2, 9)

Read the whole psalm and identify each stage. Emotions are complex and untidy when the world falls into disorder.

Listen to one woman's request to her minister: "I need to make an appointment to see you. They say Mark is dying; he may only have days left. But I know it's not true. I know he isn't dying. I need to talk to you about making arrangements for a funeral service."

If this woman didn't really believe Mark was dying, she wouldn't have begun to make plans for a service. On some level she knew he would die, but she still wanted to hold on to the hope that the disease would be reversed. These are not contradictions as much as they are small tentative steps toward compatibility with the new order of things.

In order to reach a new equilibrium, people need to walk through and not around the grief process. It is painful; it touches upon our sense of being alone as nothing else does. It hurts to be present to our own grief and to the pain of others. It is natural to want to hasten it on, to be done with it. Yet the healthy course is to persevere, to put one foot in front of the other and claim the support of others and of God's divine grace. The alternative is the development of serious spiritual, physical, and emotional distresses. Unresolved grief can manifest itself in spiritual coldness, depression, emotional illness, ulcers, and other serious problems.

For the person dying and the family and friends who are also deeply grieving, there needs to be a deep respect on the part of the caring minister for the uniqueness of each person's grief journey. Each of us will stall or advance at our own rhythm. The role of the caregiver is to offer support, not control or analysis. Being able to recognize normal and abnormal grief reactions will allow the caregiver to be a more effective companion along the way.

Normal grief reactions include the following:

- Shock

- Physical symptoms (which can be fairly immediate)

    (a) bodily distress (which can come in waves)

    (b) tightness in the throat, a choking feeling

    (c) an empty feeling in the stomach

    (d) weakness, fatigue, exhaustion

- Emotional release: crying, sighing, outbursts

- Depression: a sense of isolation, loneliness

- Guilt: what we have omitted or committed

- Panic: thinking that we see or hear the dead person.... "Am I crazy?"

- Anger, resentment, bitterness, irritability

- Helplessness, hopelessness, copelessness, restlessness, lack of concentration

- Difficulty returning to normal affairs, feeling overwhelmed

- Forgetfulness and inability to focus

- Hope returns gradually

Abnormal grief reactions include:

- No emotion, no apparent reaction, ignoring the death as if it never happened

- Throwing oneself immediately back into work and activities, burying grief

- Psychosomatic conditions: physical and mental complaints that refuse to go away even after there are no medical indications for such problems

- Personality changes: suspicious, paranoid feelings that continue without reason

- Intense unresolved anger

- Retreating from social activity, prolonged isolation

- Detrimental activity, substance abuse

- Enshrinement and idealization

- Enshrinement: for example, keeping a bedroom intact many years after a teenager died

- Idealization: glorifying the loved one and making him or her far better than in life

Be aware also that "dip-ins" will be a normal part of experience for years to come. They are the small reminders of loss that fall on the heart when a person hears a certain melody, catches sight of someone in the distance, sniffs a familiar scent, touches a fondly remembered object, or tastes a forgotten dish. These "dip-ins" may call up the sadness that will always be there, but they are also sacred moments of appreciation and joy.

We can let those who are grieving know that the experience is normal and necessary. We can invite them to share, without pushing them to talk. Gently we can reflect what we hear, listening with our hearts. We can be quiet with our care receiver. We can just be there. We can pray. We can be supportive, letting the person know we will not withdraw, yet maintaining our own boundaries. It is important that we permit the care receiver to retell the story in order to make sense of this loss. A death is never forgotten, but with time the pain softens. The deceased is a very real part of the mourner's history and by constant acknowledgment of the deceased memories flourish and even become a source of comfort.

The Minister as Healing Companion

Again we call upon our tried and true skills of listening, focusing on feelings, compatibility checking, and prayer to help us be present to a person who is dying or grieving. Here are some further strategies for patient caring:

Be there. Offering our presence during times of despair touches another's pain at a profound level. We represent God's faithfulness and love when it cannot be felt. Regular visits are necessary for quality ministry to take place.

Be sensitive to the untidiness of the process. People need to be free and comfortable with alternating between stages. They also can find comfort in a variety of expressions. On one day the dying person may need to cry and vent anger but on another might receive comfort from a favorite piece of music. There will be times when the dying or grieving person needs to be alone and other times marked by a desperate desire to be surrounded by loved ones.

Be alert to the signs of abnormal reactions. This applies primarily to grieving family and friends rather than to a dying person. If the intense reactions continue past a year, there is cause for concern. Because pastoral caregivers are not therapists or medical professionals, in such cases it is advisable to seek consultation with the pastoral care supervisor.

Provide healing resources. Many dying people desire to talk about death and their relationship with God. This is an opportunity to reflect with people on the meaning of their lives. Scripture and prayer can give expression to the deep questions and longings. The Psalms are especially supportive of the freedom to give utterance to every emotion. Scripture connects all of us with the common thread of the Judeo-Christian tradition.

When the Hebrew people found themselves in trouble or despair, they drew on the memory of God's saving acts in the past. The repetition of the stories gave the people confidence and a community call larger than the present danger. The sustaining message throughout the First Testament was "God delivered us in the past and God will deliver us again." "To you they cried, and were saved," says Psalm 22:5, "in you they trusted and were not put to shame." Jesus added to that promise as summed up in Matthew 28:20: "And remember, I am with you always to the end of the age." This captures well the source of comfort for those who are dying. They need to know that they will not be abandoned even more than believing in a last-minute cure. The pastoral caregiver can recall with the person God's self-communication both personally and communally. This, of course, will be easier for those who have given themselves to the encounter with a faith tradition. But even for those who are not so committed, this can be a time to reveal a deep connection with the Holy.

Be consistent with visits. People with long-term terminal illnesses often are forgotten, especially when they are out of sight of the local church. For those in grief, the most difficult time sets in during the weeks and months following the loss. Two weeks after a major loss is an excellent time for the pastoral caregiver to offer the quality time needed to begin the grief work in earnest.

Talk about the deceased. To be able to talk about the lost loved one promotes healing. By asking questions about the deceased, the pastoral caregiver invites the grieving individual to tell the story over again, making it real and consoling.

Provide positive feedback. Familiarity with the nature of grief will enable the caring minister to field questions and give assurance.

CARE RECEIVER: "I walked into the living room yesterday and for an instant I was certain I saw Phyllis sitting in her chair."

CARING MINISTER: "It might seem strange, but it is very normal to think we see or hear someone who has just died."

CARE RECEIVER: "Oh, what a relief. I thought I was going crazy."

One woman, recently widowed, asked the minister what exactly she could expect. She wanted information about grief, and she wanted to know what things she might do to work through her pain and loss. The minister shared that her grief journey would be unique to her and went on to enumerate many of the normal reactions that people experience.

There are many books available that can be guides and sources of comfort. One church gives each newly widowed person a copy of the book *Good Grief* by Granger Westberg. It is small, practical, and a tangible reminder of the community's continued care and support.

Conclusion

No one can walk in another's shoes or gauge the depth of sadness that results from a loss. Yet, in understanding our own grief, we can recognize some of the emotions. We can walk with people as they ache, and we can be the living reminders of God's love and care.

Spiritual Application

Martha said to Jesus, "Lord, if you had been here, my brother would not have died. But even now I know that God will give you whatever you ask." Jesus said to her, "Your brother will rise again." Martha said to him, "I know that he will rise again in the resurrection on the last day." Jesus said to her, "I am the resurrection and the life. Those who believe in me, even though they die, will live, and everyone who lives and believes in me will never die. Do you believe this?" (John 11:21–26)

Jesus had a beautiful way of entering every human scene fully and honestly, always meeting people where they were. In this story, he enters a scene of grief and of aching questions: "Why didn't Jesus arrive in time? Why didn't he heal Lazarus, their brother?"

The response of Jesus is noteworthy. There is no recrimination for any doubts they have. Jesus is so moved by everyone's grief, his spirit so troubled, that he weeps with them. St. Paul would reiterate that wisdom in his letter to the Romans when he said, "Rejoice with those who rejoice, weep with those who weep." A Benedictine sister friend of mine says, "Remember, Paul didn't say, 'Cheer up those who weep,' but, 'Weep with those who weep.'"

Jesus had the ability to meet people where they were. He gave thousands of people bread and fish when they were hungry. He turned water into wine at a wedding just to save a young man and woman from the lifelong stigma of being known as that couple from Cana who ran out of wine at their wedding. He took children on his knee and talked with women as if they were capable of understanding his teachings.

Because of his ability to be so fully immersed and involved in everyday concerns, people were able to hear his messages and his teachings that pointed to "something greater than" the human scene. He spoke to a woman at a well about living water that would satisfy a longing much deeper than mere thirst. In this passage he says, "Martha, do you know that Lazarus will rise again; do you know that anyone with faith will live forever?"

Especially interesting is Jesus' response to Martha's reference to the resurrection on the last day or the end of time. Perhaps it was the cliché of the day, just as we would say, "Oh, I know he's in a better place and I'll see him in heaven." But Jesus doesn't go with that train of thought. Instead, he brings Martha back to the present implications of the resurrection. She is invited to grasp the transcendent meaning in the current moment. Martha is being formed by this experience, and it has moved her toward her unique faith statement.

Grief is a call to encounter Christ's living presence in the chaos of the trauma. The promise of afterlife is no doubt very consoling, but it is not enough. God always seizes the immediate occasion as the opportune time of transformation.

Pray with the above passage using the *lectio divina* method.

Read. Review the narrative and imagine all the unspoken things Martha was thinking as she ran to Jesus. *Silence (two minutes minimum)*.

Reflect. Think about a time in your life when God didn't respond as you hoped. What did you say or want to say to God? *Silence*.

Respond. Name any transforming outcomes of the loss or trauma. What were the moments of resurrection along the way? *Silence.*

Rest. As you recall the occasion, offer it up to the Mystery once more. *Silence (up to twenty minutes).*

Ministry with the Wisdom People

> *If you have gathered nothing in your youth,*
> *how can you find anything in your old age?*
> *How fine a thing: sound judgement with grey hairs,*
> *and for greybeards to know how to advise!*
> *How fine a thing: wisdom in the aged,*
> *and considered advice coming from people of distinction!*
> *The crown of the aged is ripe experience,*
> *their glory, the fear of the Lord.* (Ecclus. 25:3–6 NJB)

"Elderly," "age-gifted," "senior citizens," "aging," "chronologically gifted," and "the third age" are just a few of the terms we have come to use for persons in later life. Some churches have adopted the label "Wisdom People" and have found it to be accepted with enthusiasm by this age group. It expresses the integrity, experience, uniqueness, and often hidden value of this growing and complex population. The epithet "Wisdom People" reminds us that our respect is well placed for a generation that still has much to give as well as receive. As recently as the early 1980s the term "elderly" was used to describe an adult as young as seventy-two. But now "elderly" is reserved for the very aged and frail. With better health care and lifestyle advances, this population has earned further divisions of identification. In *Ministry with Older Persons*, Arthur Becker has defined three distinct phases of the third age: the *young old*, age sixty-five to seventy-three; the *middle old*, those seventy-three to eighty, and the *frail elderly*, who are over eighty and unable to live safely on their own. There are many exceptions to this general guideline. We can probably name persons in their nineties who are independent and energetic and ones in their seventies who are frail and require total care. However, the division is useful in preventing us from lumping all people over sixty-five into one category. They are as diverse a group as any in our society.

For the purposes of this chapter, we will be turning our attention to those undergoing crisis or the diminishment that comes with aging. It is not designed to be a comprehensive treatment of all the issues facing the aging but a summary to prompt reflection and understanding. Pastoral ministry with this group requires familiarity with the losses and gains accompanying change. As the list unfolds, we will be able to see God's grace working in both the positive and negative experiences. Both can provide the richest soil on which to test our faith.

General Shared Experience of Growing Older

Losses and diminishments are commonly experienced in the following areas:

Physical Decline

- weakening of all five senses
- reduction of mobility and muscle strength
- perception that physical attractiveness wanes
- onset of chronic disease such as arthritis and diabetes
- possible acute conditions such as cancer, heart disease, stroke

Interpersonal Losses

- death of spouses, friends, children, pets
- divorce
- loss of family role

Social and Identity Shifts

- retirement, loss of worthwhile work or title
- loss of church or community leadership roles
- transition from being a helper to one who needs help

Decreased Independence

- loss of initiative and control
- loss of transportation
- move from home to facility
- reduced or fixed income
- personal safety at risk
- decision making taken over by others

On the other hand, there can be **gains and consolations,** namely:

Increased Freedom and Available Time

- for exploration of new creative outlets
- for volunteering in church or community
- for prayer and spiritual deepening
- for enjoyment of leisure and travel
- for enjoyment of family, grandchildren

New Responsibilities

- as a font of wisdom
- as a sharer of experience
- as a bearer of history and tradition
- as a provider of spiritual guidance
- as a source of generativity* and mentoring

This list is by no means exhaustive. But it gives us pause to consider the enormity of losses that many in our parishes have sustained. Notice also that a loss for one may be a consolation for another.

---

*Passing on to the next generation.

Susan may be devastated by the end of a satisfying career, while Cynthia is ecstatic that she has the time to turn to that trunk of half-finished quilts. Sixty-five-year-old Richard may now be able to fulfill a leadership role on the vestry or parish council, but eighty-year-old Harry knows he no longer has the stamina to volunteer one day a week at the food bank.

The last cycle of life can be, for the Christian, a time of harvesting a lifetime of full, faithful living. Wisdom People have received God's grace through joys and sorrows, increasing and decreasing, knowing and unknowing, consolations and desolations.

Foundations for Pastoral Care

While it is essential to recognize and understand the losses and gains of the third age, on an even deeper level these experiences mirror the twofold movements of the spiritual journey. Many great writers have described these complementary paths, which derive their wisdom from Jesus in the Gospels. Two authors who have articulated it particularly well for our application are Pierre Teilhard de Chardin and W. H. Vanstone.

In *The Divine Milieu* Teilhard describes transformation into Christ by two modalities: our activities and our passivities. It is easy to accept the divine action operating in and through the areas of life which are under our control, direction, initiative, and capacity to nurture. We fashion our lives and set our course, inviting God to be our companion, guide, revealer, and sustainer. But what happens when outside forces oppose our efforts, seize control, and we suddenly become the passive one left to react to an untimely interruption? The Gospels challenge the believer to embrace these passivities over which we have no control as the learning edges of our faith. Jesus did not preach a Gospel of avoidance or of protection from the human condition, but one in which we will never be separated from God. Ours is not a faith of escape from difficulties but one that offers the inner resources to turn a depreciative event into an appreciation of God's unfailing presence.

Teilhard drew his insight from the observation that we are formed to an equal extent by those things that we control (activities) and by the events we cannot control (passivities). He saw these small "deaths" or diminishments, which begin as hostile forces, as opportunities for transformation, provided the believer trusts in God. He expressed his thanksgiving for the redemption of what we view as uninvited and chaotic when he prayed, "Yes, O God, I believe it; and I believe it more willingly because it is not only a question of my being consoled but of my being completed."*

In a more recent treatment of the same theme, W. H. Vanstone applies the two threads of activity and passivity explicitly to the process of aging. He uses the passion of Jesus as a pattern for the task of the final years. Jesus had been the initiator and director of his ministry; he called, he taught, he healed. At the Last Supper, Jesus announced the closure of his active ministry. He was retiring from what those around him regarded as his "meaningful work." The Last Supper was not, however, the last chapter or the end of the story. The dramatic turn of events at his arrest would reveal Jesus' reactions under the stress of loss, of being handed over to outside powers. His freedom to act and move about on his own was snatched away and his friends regarded him as a failure. It would not be until after the resurrection that they would be able to place meaning on his suffering and death.

His revelation to us of divine activity was not defined solely by his work as a preacher, teacher, and healer, but even more by his response in the darkest moments of grief and loss. Jesus was not complete until he confronted the forces of evil on the most personal level. Jesus did not make his final announcement until he was dying on the cross. "It is finished" alluded not only to his final breath but to the completion of his mission and life purpose. His helplessness became holiness as he freely chose to remain on the cross for a higher purpose.

Vanstone suggests that the frail elderly who live in the in-between time from work to death are indeed living out their own form of passion. This has the potential of completing their formation into the image of Christ. This thoroughly healthy and redemptive posture can prevent us from dismissing this time of diminishment as unproductive or bereft of meaning.

---

*Pierre Teilhard de Chardin, *The Divine Milieu* (New York: Harper & Row, 1960), 78.

Role of the Caregiver

The church and more specifically the pastoral caregivers have the task of providing spiritual resources to those living in the in-between time. Those desiring to be more effective caring ministers to the Wisdom People can benefit from adopting an attitude that recognizes (1) that the story is not yet over and (2) that usefulness does not define value.

Appreciation of the Story

Many older adults love to tell their life story. Longevity has given them more memories to share, and for many the happiest years are behind them. The present may not hold many interesting prospects or anticipations. Memories, however, affirm a sense of self-worth. There are even deeper reasons for reminiscence. Life review becomes one of the vital tasks of this phase of life. People who are able to look back at their lives as a whole can see them as a tapestry woven with the threads of joy and sorrow, birth and death, attachment and detachment, increasing and decreasing. They can recall times when God's providence was manifested, and remembering God's strength in difficult times can affirm that God will continue the divine activity until the last. Through their stories the Wisdom People send their messages and reveal their identities. The caring minister who listens with the heart to this holy narrative is able to look past the pale, wrinkled skin, the gray hair, and the scaled-down environment to see the smart, funny, capable, and kind contributing individual who still exists.

For example, the ninety-two-year-old man who tells his visitor week after week about his success in business and knowledge of "who's who" is not so much imparting information as conveying his unique identity. Caring ministers need to be alert to stories and dig a little deeper for the treasure hidden in the message. Knowing the story and the message can help the minister to connect the past with the present circumstances and see the wisdom being revealed.

Usefulness versus Value

Our Western culture still abides by the principle that usefulness and productivity are the true measures of worth. "Doing" is prized above "being," even though our Judeo-Christian legacy teaches otherwise. We are hard pressed to recall any incidents from Jesus' life when he praised the most productive, powerful, and aggressive of his day. Instead he pointed to the most useless, the weakest, and the least powerful as the models of the Kingdom of God. Their total dependency on God was their gift and their path to divine union.

Many of the older generation cannot see any value to their lives apart from continuing activity. It is easy for the Wisdom People to feel useless to the Christian community once their volunteer work is finished and they have nothing to show at the end of the day. But this is where our faith can shine the brightest. Wisdom People are, after all, still full-time human beings. Caring ministers enjoy the privilege of valuing them by a ministry of listening and presence. Regular visits assure people they are not forgotten, their work counted for something, and they count even more as valuable members of the faith community. They can now be relied upon for their prayers, their oral histories, and the benefit of their wisdom and experience.

Practical Strategies for Ministry

The foundations of listening and focusing on feelings discussed in earlier chapters will of course be essential in this ministry. Additional patience and understanding is required for those whose senses and responses might have slowed down.

• Treat the older generation as peers who deserve respect. They are after all our Wisdom People. It is all too common for professionals, institutions, and adult children to fall into the habit of talking to older adults as if they were children, using age clichés ("You are no spring chicken") and talking in sing-song voices. A physical disability does not assume the inability to make wise decisions. Older people need to be given any opportunity to make choices, even very small ones.

• Be assertive in what you will or will not do for them. Many caring ministers are able and pleased to assist the person with practical needs such as reading mail or providing transportation. But others cannot or choose not to provide such assistance and may be able to point them in the direction of local resources. In either case the pastoral caregiver and the older adult need to establish a mutual understanding of each other's needs and limitations. Again, approach such a discussion as adult to adult.

• Don't avoid difficult subjects such as their own death or their guilt over the past. The caring minister may be the only one who takes the time to listen to the deep questions and longings. The stark confrontation with realities can flow into a sacred time of sharing and peace making.

• Be prepared to receive as much as you give. The Wisdom People are paving the way through passion time before us. These mothers and fathers of faith are living proof that Christianity works. Many caring ministers have arrived with the motive to help but have found that they themselves have received unexpected inspiration and strength.

• Allow them to do something tangible for you if they wish. Accept the cup of coffee or the small gift appreciatively. It is important for them to be in the position of giving.

• Regard each loss, no matter how small, seriously and compassionately. It is a mistake to assume that people become accustomed to loss after loss. It is more accurate to regard diminishments as compounding upon one another. Something that might seem insignificant to us may be the blow that causes a person to totter on the edge of despair.

• Believe in their ability to change and grow. The human spirit often needs a gentle urging to release its dormant powers.

Consider Myrtle, who recovered beautifully from a major stroke only to suffer a much smaller one a few months later. The woman from the church who had become her pastoral care minister noticed when she saw her in the hospital that Myrtle was being treated by the staff in a condescending manner. Myrtle, ninety years old and legally blind, was understandably agitated and confused in her unfamiliar surroundings. The nurse and the much younger patient in the next bed rolled their eyes at her confused, tearful, and angry statements. The caring minister was able to soothe her by taking each remark seriously and by gently trying to acquaint Myrtle with the rehabilitation unit. The caring minister then talked to the therapist and asked her about the plan for Myrtle and, in particular, about teaching her to walk again.

THERAPIST: "Oh, she can't walk. We don't intend to try."

CARING MINISTER: "I know Myrtle was walking in no time after her last stroke. I bet she will surprise you. She was a great walker all her life, and I know it will come back."

THERAPIST: "Her stroke is too extensive, and she is not co-operating."

The caring minister, who had become Myrtle's sole support system, would not accept this prognosis and was instrumental in getting Myrtle moved to the health care facility that had been so successful after the first stroke. Back among familiar people, Myrtle relaxed, and her agitation subsided. By the end of her first full day, not only was she walking without assistance, but with some help she climbed a ladder and placed a sticker of Garfield the cat on the ceiling of the therapy room. Two years later, Myrtle still walks without a cane. How many others, not so fortunate, remain bedridden because no one believes in them?

Conclusion

Not everyone will be called or called upon to minister to the older generation. This chapter can provide insight and opportunities to reflect upon the losses, gains, and crises that occur at any age. It is a useful exercise for all of us to examine our own attitudes toward the aging and about our own aging process. We are now being formed into what we shall become.

Spiritual Application

Is it plausible that the rhythm of *lectio divina* that leads to Centering Prayer and the contemplative dimension is much more than a prayer method? In an earlier chapter I correlated the steps of *lectio divina* with pastoral care. This application goes even further. Conceivably the long-term durability and success of *lectio divina* is precisely that it repeats the normal life cycle of a human being. It is a microcosm of our normal development on the spiritual, physical, and psychological paths of life. Its very efficacy as a prayer method may be due in part to a subconscious pull toward the repetition of the dance of life (from increasing to decreasing, from acquisition to letting go, and from awareness to awe).

I was fascinated to observe the same theme and rhythm in the Scripture passage quoted earlier from Ecclesiasticus (Sirach). (I've taken some liberty in the interpretation of verse 4 in assuming that sound judgment can come about only through a full encounter with life.) Compare these couplets with the *lectio divina* steps of Read, Reflect, Respond, Rest (as shown on the facing page) and consider how they relate to the human task of growth.

For the pastoral caregiver awe will serve far better than tidy endings. For some, whose suffering cannot be cured, healing comes from the collaboration of our faith, our hope, and our belief in things not seen and in God's unfailing divine love. Our presence is critical as words recede into silence.

Lectio Divina — *Reading Scripture as Prayer*	Ecclesiasticus 25:3–6	Human Development as Contemplative Journey
Read the story in God's Word (lectio): Be present to the Word. Listen to the story for information. Take it in. Get acquainted with the passage of Scripture.	If you have gathered nothing in your youth, how can you find anything in your old age?	Youth is the time in life to learn, grow, increase, receive, gather information. Listen to life; take it in.
Reflect (meditatio): Become actively involved with the story. *Pay attention to what attracts your attention.* Notice your own feelings. Reflect on your own inner experience of the Scripture. Allow the Gospels to be a mirror of your own life.	How fine a thing: sound judgement with grey hairs, and for greybeards to know how to advise!	With increased knowledge the unique person is emerging. The person begins to reflect and imagine the direction of life. Judgments and decisions are being formed.
Respond (oratio): Be free to express what is pouring out of the reflection — praise, tears, repentance, thanksgiving. How is God becoming formed in you? Celebrate this with thanksgiving.	How fine a thing: wisdom in the aged, And considered advice coming from people of distinction.	Knowledge, experience, learning, and selfhood bear the fruit of wisdom. God is forming and transforming the individual. The person is capable of empowering others and is responsive to the rest of the world.
Rest (contemplatio): Let go of all reflections and responses in order to allow God to speak to you in the mystery of silence and quiet presence. Surrender to the mystery and awe.	The crown of the aged is ripe experience, their glory, the fear [awe] of the Lord.	Ripe experience and wisdom lead to a posture of awe, not absolutes toward God and life. The last phase is lived more as an appreciation of mystery than the need to have all the answers. All of life reaches its summit in contemplation.

Care during Crisis

But we have this treasure in clay jars, so that it may be made clear that this extraordinary power belongs to God and does not come from us. We are afflicted in every way, but not crushed; perplexed, but not driven to despair; persecuted, but not forsaken; struck down but not destroyed; always carrying in the body the death of Jesus, so that the life of Jesus may also be made visible in our bodies. (2 Cor. 4:7–10)

Crises come in many forms. The six o'clock news reports a barrage of critical events. Even the sports and weather segments cannot escape the harsh reality of the human condition. Consider the wide variety of events that fling people's orderly lives into instant disorder:

- The Olympic favorite missteps, falls, and loses her chance for a medal.

- At a home wedding reception, a gas grill explodes completely destroying the house of the newlywed couple.

- A healthy, active sixty-three-year-old woman falls down the basement steps and never regains consciousness.

- A young wife and mother discovers her husband's infidelity.

- Floods overtake the Midwest and many homes and businesses are destroyed.

- A newly retired man suffers a sudden episode of glaucoma, leaving one eye sightless and the other 80 percent diminished.

- In a senseless drive-by shooting, an innocent three-year-old boy is killed.

We can go on recounting with hundreds of unexpected occurrences that disrupt the lives of individuals, families, communities, countries, and the world. Whether confined to a household or affecting the globe, they share the signs of trauma and they require the same caring responses if people are to regain balance and the strength to reorder life.

Reactions to Crisis

A crisis turns the world upside down. It has the effect of making people feel disconnected, separated, and scattered. Its victims would like to be able to push the rewind button of life, return to the instant before the crisis happened, and somehow change events. Unfortunately that is not possible, and instead they are forced into circumstances that will call upon every strength that can be mustered. In an earlier chapter we mentioned the reactions of shock, numbness, and disbelief. Here are further reactions to unexpected devastation:

terror	sorrow and sadness	confusion
fear	frustration	feeling of fragility
rage	indecisiveness	feeling of abandonment
denial	guilt and remorse	feeling of disablement
panic	shame	feeling of powerlessness

In situations of crisis all normal people experience these feelings to some extent. Even Job, who was a man of trust and integrity, cried out in his distress and voiced his doubts and feelings to God. His cries were the foundation of his dialogue and his confrontation with God. This would in the end reveal his enlarged view of the divine activity in his own personal life and in the universe.

Peter, who was privileged to walk with Jesus and who enjoyed the benefit of his daily teachings, was instantly caught in the grip of separation from all that gave his life meaning. His path was excruciating. He faced all the inner demons of denial and terror. Yet it was in that very darkness that he relinquished egocentricity and was then able to receive a lasting strength and power. Both Job and Peter would have their lives given back to them, and each would experience a turning point resulting in restored hope.

A crisis is a turning point. In a medical crisis the disease or condition has reached an apex. The outcome can go either way: either the fever will break or the patient will die. The Greek root word *krei,* from which "crisis" is derived, means to separate, sift, discern. Times of danger, trouble, and devastation become the decisive, crucial periods when events can take a turn for better or for worse.

The Healing Role of the Caring Minister

There are times of unexpected, sudden crisis, when we are called upon to exert unusual emotional, physical, and spiritual strengths. This comes when we are least able to do so. Most emergencies demand immediate action, swift decision making, and clarity of direction. The very reactions to crisis mentioned earlier make it almost impossible to respond without the care and support of others. One of the key elements that will determine if the route taken will enable recovery is the presence of a companion along the way. Caring ministers have the strategic advantage on the scene of a crisis because they are not swept up into the paralyzing reactions. Our pastoral response can be divided into three categories: what to be, what to do, and planting seeds of hope.

What to Be

Be there. Our presence is the greatest gift of our ministry. People may remember little of what we say, but they will never forget the people who simply sat with them. Just imagine how disconnected a person feels from reality without the physical presence of another human being. Our presence is a deep consolation in and of itself.

Be flexible. Events and moods will change almost moment by moment. Be prepared to "go with the flow," taking action at one point and being comfortable with long silences at another.

Be familiar with their vulnerabilities. Become thoroughly acquainted with the list of reactions to crisis. This will sensitize you to all of the feelings of fragility and threat the care receivers are undergoing and will help diffuse any fear you might have.

Be a listener. Let the person vent rage, frustration, disbelief. It is an important beginning to the process of healing. Honor those expressions, but remember this is not the time to get into in-depth focusing on feelings. That will come later.

Be Christ's presence. St. Teresa wrote that Christ has no body now but ours. To a great extent we are the vessels through which grace is mediated. Our presence reminds people that they can count on the faith community, and it sends the message that God can be counted on as well.

What to Do

Take action. I'll never forget the report to our caring ministry class by a man who was satisfied that he'd mastered "The Gift of Listening" (chapter 3) and "Focus on Feelings" (chapter 4 and 5). He was on a hike with his mountain club when one of the hikers fell and broke her foot. Full of compassion and newly acquired skills, he bent over and asked her how she was feeling about what just happened. She grabbed him by the collar and screamed, "Get me off this mountain!" Indeed, there is a time and a place for everything under heaven, and that was not the time for inner exploration. Crises generally demand action, not words. The pastoral caregiver will probably be called upon to *act:* make telephone calls, give hugs, make coffee, get soup, answer the door. Try to attend to the very basic, functional survival needs of the care receiver. Self-actualization and active reflection come later.

Stand by to protect. Your judgment will be more sound than the care receiver's. Watch out for self-destructive behaviors, and gently steer away outside forces that might be further disruptive. Intervene, but do not interfere.

Assist with decisions. The operative word is "assist." You can be the calm, clear voice that names the options and suggested order of procedures. For instance: "What do you think about the doctor's suggestion of surgery?" instead of "I think you should try it or you'll never know."

Assist with resources. Many times people do not know or cannot recall at the time who to call for what. You can bring order into disorder by assisting them with procedures like calling the church, the pastor, the mortuary, the police, or helping out with whatever circumstances require.

Planting Seeds of Hope

Strength of community. In most crises, people reach out for help. That first act is an unspoken acknowledgment that there is indeed strength outside of ourselves. It is the first act of trust that helps pave the path to healing.

Love casts out fear. The presence of the caring ministry is a profound reception of God's love by the care receiver. Just as all the other energies are tapped into, so is love. Our silent and spoken prayers will deflate fear.

Opportunity for Providence. When people's worlds collapse, they are shaken to their very core and cannot confront the deep issues of life. They remind us of what is eternal and lasting. The seeds of lasting faith, hope, and love are often planted in the early hours following a trauma. Who was there? What was said and done? Who sat in the silence, read from a Psalm, or uttered a simple prayer? These events all become snapshots in the heart to be treasured and remembered.

Enter the mystery. Crises take us fully into the territory of God's mysterious love. When there are no answers, we must give up the useless device of analysis and open ourselves to that which we cannot control. Slowly we feel a lifting, catch a glimmer of joy, receive an insight, or appreciate a memory. We cannot create these experiences by an act of will, but we can openly receive them as a gift from the Beloved.

Conclusion

Crises are indeed opportunities for heightening our awareness of the human condition and discovering wellsprings of hope and unfathomed depths of God's love. The caring minister can be the one most instrumental in helping people to find the beautiful new patterns for living.

∽⟨⟩∾

We are afflicted in every way, but not crushed; perplexed, but not forsaken; struck down, but not destroyed. (2 Cor. 4:8–9)

Spiritual Application

Now on that same day two of them were going to a village called Emmaus, about seven miles from Jerusalem, and talking with each other about all these things that had happened. While they were talking and discussing, Jesus himself came near and went with them, but their eyes were kept from recognizing him. And he said to them, "What are you discussing with each other while you walk along?" They stood still, looking sad. Then one of them, whose name was Cleopas, answered him, "Are you the only stranger in Jerusalem who does not know the things that have taken place there in these days?" He asked them, "What things?" They replied, "The things about Jesus of Nazareth, who was a prophet mighty in deed and word before God and all the people, and how our chief priests and leaders handed him over to be condemned to death and crucified him. But we had hoped that he was the one to redeem Israel. Yes, and besides all this, it is now the third day since these things took place. Moreover, some women of our group astounded us. They were at the tomb early this morning, and when they did not find his body there, they came back and told us that they had indeed seen a vision of angels who said that he was alive. Some of those who were with us went to the tomb and found it just as the women had said; but they did not see him." Then he said to them, "Oh, how foolish you are, and how slow of heart to believe all that the prophets have declared! Was it not necessary that the Messiah should suffer these things and then enter into his glory?" Then beginning with Moses and all the prophets, he interpreted to them the things about himself in all the Scriptures.

As they came near the village to which they were going, he walked ahead as if he were going on. But they urged him strongly, saying, "Stay with us, because it is almost evening and the day is now nearly over." So he went in to stay with them. When he was at the table with them, he took bread, blessed and broke it, and gave it to them. Then their eyes were opened, and they recognized him; and he vanished from their sight. They said to each other, "Were not our hearts burning within us while he was talking to us on the road, while he was opening the scriptures to us?"

(Luke 24:13–32)

We enter the scene of a crisis. Two of the disciples are traveling, for some reason, away from the others. They have become separated. They are so highly focused on their grief that it has overtaken their power even to recognize the risen Jesus. Jesus begins his ministry to them by inviting them to tell their story. We can feel their pain and sense their preoccupation with their own dashed hopes: "We had hoped that he was the one to redeem Israel." Jesus reconnects them to their own faith tradition, reminding them of prophesy and the fulfillment of God's plan.

Yet they remain blind to his identity until he repeats a ritual with which they are familiar. They recognize him in concrete, tangible species. At the very point of recognition, he disappears but leaves them with a new strength and an experience to treasure, to share, and to add to the faith formation of an entire church.

People in trauma, shock, and confusion find it difficult to access or even to recognize the sources of help available to them. Even the most devout will fail to recognize God's grace and activity. But like Cleopas and his companion, they will realize what has happened later as the events are remembered: "Were not our hearts burning within us while he was talking to us on the road?"

As we reflect on this passage and the story of recovery for the infant church, one reality stands out above all others. Resurrection did not rewind history to where it had been prior to the crucifixion. Even the resurrected Christ continued to display the wounds he suffered. Life was restored but not duplicated. Jesus would not be physically part of their everyday lives. They lost their fishing buddy, teacher, healer, son, brother, friend. It was not until he finally vanished and ascended that they turned a corner and received the power through the Holy Spirit to become leaders and Christ's witnesses.

Healing after a crisis is not about going back and duplicating what was. It is going forward and discovering new forms and patterns for living. We might compare our lives to a kaleidoscope. At every turn the pattern changes. It is impossible to turn the barrel backward and find the same colors and shapes exactly as they were. But the new patterns are beautiful and different.

ᨀ Chapter 11

Substance Abuse

by Anonymous

> *They came to the other side of the sea, to the country of the Gerasenes. And when he had stepped out of the boat, immediately a man out of the tombs with an unclean spirit met him. He lived among the tombs; and no one could restrain him any more, even with a chain; for he had often been restrained with shackles and chains, but the chains he wrenched apart, and the shackles he broke in pieces; and no one had the strength to subdue him. Night and day among the tombs and on the mountains he was always howling and bruising himself with stones. When he saw Jesus from a distance, he ran and bowed down before him; and he shouted at the top of his voice, "What have you to do with me, Jesus, Son of the Most High God? I adjure you by God, do not torment me." For he had said to him, "Come out of the man, you unclean spirit." Then Jesus asked him, "What is your name?" He replied, "My name is Legion; for we are many.... As he was getting into the boat, the man who had been possessed by demons begged him that he might be with him."*   (Mark 5:1–9, 18)

These verses from Mark could easily have been written about alcoholism (or other drug abuse). Let me take these verses apart and illustrate my meaning.

> *And when he stepped out of the boat, immediately a man out of the tombs with an unclean spirit met him ... the man who had been possessed by demons....*

We can think of the disease of alcoholism as an unclean spirit or a demon. The man, aware and made miserable by his sickness, approaches Jesus.

He lived among the tombs; and no one could restrain him....

We choose to be bitterly, unhappily alone even though we may be surrounded by family. By our anger, our excuses, and our denial we ignore defensively the pleas and animosity of others who despair of our behavior.

Night and day among the tombs and on the mountains he was always howling and bruising himself....

Many times we are loud and obnoxious when we are drinking or drugging. The results of our addiction are physical, emotional, and spiritual bruising.

When he saw Jesus from a distance, he ran and bowed down before him....

After recognizing his illness and from whence his help would come, the man ran and bowed down to the Lord.

My name is Legion; for we are many.

In the world there are millions of alcoholics, both recovering and those unfortunates still using this drug.

In simple terms, an addiction, whether it be to a person, place, or thing, takes precedence in one's life to the exclusion of anyone or anything else. Those with an addiction to alcohol or other drugs put the importance of these substances foremost regardless of how detrimental to their lives or to the lives around them. Threats or pleas; loss of family, jobs, friends, self-esteem; material, legal, physical, emotional, moral problems — nothing seems to matter to the addict. Finding, hiding, and using the drug of choice outweighs everything else in the addict's existence.

Halting this personal destruction does not come from simply wishing it away. It is not a moral problem or a choice of will power. In 1975 the American Psychiatric Association concluded that alcoholism is a disease, and in 1990 the following definition was approved by the board of directors of the National Council on Alcoholism and Drug Dependence and the American Society of Addiction Medicine:

Alcoholism is a primary disease with genetic, psychosocial, and environmental factors influencing its development and manifestations. The disease is often progressive and fatal. It is characterized by continuous or periodic: impaired control over drinking, preoccupation with the drug alcohol, use of alcohol despite adverse consequences, and distortions in thinking, most notably denial.

There is no magic pill that will take away this illness. Total abstinence from alcohol or any other addictive drug is the only known solution to stop the progression of the disease; it is not curable, but it can be arrested for a lifetime if one never again picks up a drink or a drug. It is rare now in the 1990s that a person uses only alcohol. Most of the population comes with an addiction to several drugs, and since there seems to be a cross-tolerance from one substance to another, abstinence from all drugs is necessary for sobriety. Reintroducing any addictive substance into one's system eventually leads back to the use of the favored drug.

The alcoholic comes from all backgrounds, all religions, both sexes, all ages, all economic situations, all types of employment from school janitor to CEO. Only 3 to 5 percent of the alcoholic population is on skid row. We are in school, we attend church, and we have jobs. We are teenagers and younger; we are your parents and your grandparents. You will find us on the golf course, playing in bridge tournaments, exercising in weight rooms, eating or cooking in restaurants, attending the theater or movies, and being cast in plays and films. We are your dentists, doctors, nurses, lawyers, judges, police officers, politicians, priests and ministers, therapists. We are in all professions. We are esteemed family men and women, the pillars of the churches, or we may be social outcasts without employment. We are everywhere in society. We have babies with Fetal Alcohol Syndrome. We drink and drive, causing 50 percent of driving fatalities and a great percentage of lethal one-car accidents. Some statistics report that 90 percent of us in the jail and prison population have alcohol- or other drug-induced crimes. Yet many of us can function, hide our addiction, and even look good for a time. Some of us never alert the legal system, never are cited for a drinking-driving offense, never are jailed, and never are hospitalized. However, in all cases, we pay an incredibly high price in personal, spiritual, emotional, and physical losses.

Alcohol is the most widely used drug in this country. One-fourth of all American homes are affected. Women are more quickly overwhelmed by alcohol than men because of a lower quantity of the stomach enzyme necessary to digest alcohol. Women are more often prescribed legal psychoactive drugs by physicians, usually resulting in dependency on several substances. There is a genetic predisposition to alcoholism. Children of alcoholics have a four times greater risk of developing this disease than children of nonalcoholics.

Alcohol is a depressant drug. It acts like a tranquilizer. It is classified as a sedative-hypnotic. At the onset of drinking it may appear that one is on a stimulant. This is because reason and intellect vanish, and one is left with uninhibited emotion allowing one to do foolish, sometimes dangerous deeds. As more alcohol is consumed, mood changes occur. A person can be angry, depressed, or happy, loud or quiet. The alcoholic can vomit, pass out, or black out (a state wherein alcoholics seem to be functioning but have no knowledge or memory of their actions, a condition that can last minutes, hours, or days). Alcohol supersedes hunger, and many alcoholics are malnourished.

Because denial is such a common symptom of this disease, alcoholics may be the last one to admit to the problem. They live in a solitary loneliness confined in a tunnel of despair and self-loathing. Yet it seems impossible for them to imagine a day without drinking. The family also is captured in this trap of disavowal and many times refuses to name the sickness. This is, indeed, a family illness, and as the drinking continues everyone is infected. Those members not using a drug assume unhealthy roles and become frantic in their attempts to contain and control the disease. Isolated by choice, hoping to conceal their problems from the world, they each take part in this masquerade as feelings of anger, guilt, extreme sadness, and fear abound. The toll on everyone is dramatic, and these emotions do not diminish quickly even if the alcoholic becomes sober. Help is necessary for everyone, whether it be through Alcoholics Anonymous/Al-Anon, therapy, or a combination of both.

There are some signs and symptoms that accompany the disease of alcoholism, although these may not be experienced by all addicts every time they use their drug of choice.

- preoccupation with alcohol (when, where, and how to get it)

- increased tolerance (more alcohol needed to get drunk)

- gulping drinks

- drinking alone

- using alcohol as a medication (for anxiety, sleep, etc.)

- blackouts

- protecting the supply

- loss of control (inability to stop drinking after having set a limit)

- changing types of liquor (from gin to bourbon to beer)

- "going on the wagon"

- sneaking drinks, hiding one's bottle

- lying about how much one drinks

- drinking in the morning

- changing friends and places to drink

- unbalanced diet, poor eating habits

- medical problems

- shaking, hallucinating, convulsing when withdrawing from alcohol

Some of the common excuses, rationalizations, or justifications alcoholics use include:

- I only drink beer (or wine, etc.).

- I only drink to unwind.

- It wasn't alcohol that made me sick ... it was.

- I can stop anytime I want to.

- I can drive better when I've had a drink.

- I only drink on weekends.

- I can handle it.

- If you had a spouse, job, etc., like I do, you would drink too.

- I work hard. I deserve a drink.

If a person uses an excuse to justify or rationalize drinking, it is generally an indication of an alcohol problem.

For most people who finally admit to their addiction, the most successful program is Alcoholics Anonymous (AA). Let me give a little background. In 1935, a New York stockbroker, Bill W., and an Akron physician, Dr. Bob, met and realized, after telling each other their past drinking stories, that to stay sober they needed to share their "experience, strength, and hope" with other alcoholics. Thus Alcoholics Anonymous was born. Small groups sprang up in Akron and New York City, and in 1939 a hundred recovering men and women came together and wrote a book called *Alcoholics Anonymous,* which we refer to as "The Big Book." In the first 164 pages along with Bill's story there are accounts illustrating the hopelessness of alcoholism and the methods employed to avoid, ignore, or fix this problem. Chapter 5 offers the "Twelve Steps," the cornerstone of this program. These Steps seem divinely inspired since they have continued to remain fresh and workable throughout the years. Suggestions on how to work these steps, information for the family, ways to reach the agnostic, and the incredible promises offered to us who complete the step work, fill the first section. The remainder of "The Big Book" is devoted to personal stories of men and women who faced their alcoholism and willingly shared their "experience, strength, hope, and recovery." Although AA is not a religious fellowship, there is a spiritual foundation that reaches most people of all religious persuasions who are ready to admit to this disease and genuinely want help. Many other programs that seek to aid people with other addictions have adopted these steps, as they seem to have a universal usefulness for recovery.

The preamble to *Alcoholics Anonymous* perhaps best explains this program:

Alcoholics Anonymous is a fellowship of men and women who share their experience, strength and hope with each other that they may solve their common problem and help others to recover from alcoholism. The only requirement for membership is a desire to stop drinking. There are no dues or fees for AA membership; we are self supporting through our own contributions. AA is not allied with any sect, denomination, politics, organization or institution; does not wish to engage in any controversy, neither endorses nor opposes any causes. Our primary purpose is to stay sober and help other alcoholics.*

We try for "spiritual progress, not perfection" in working the twelve steps. These guidelines, by which we attempt to live, give us a wonderful basis for remaining sober. In essence, we admit we can't handle our alcoholism, we ask for God's help, we clean up our side of the street, we stay honest, making amends immediately, we look to our Higher Power or God for direction, and then we try to help others.

With the twelve suggested steps to recovery outlined in chapter 5 of "The Big Book," I have chosen Scripture verses. These steps are our gift, yet they can be used by anyone for a fuller, more spiritual life. Although alcohol or drug addiction may not be your problem, all of us suffer from "addictions" of some kind.

1. **We admitted we were powerless over alcohol — that our lives had become unmanageable.**

   "For I know that nothing good dwells within me, that is, in my flesh. I can will what is right, but I cannot do it. For I do not do the good I want, but the evil I do not want is what I do." (Rom. 7:18–19)

Alcoholics Anonymous, 3d ed. (New York: Alcoholics Anonymous World Services, 1976). The Twelve Steps of Alcoholics Anonymous have been reprinted with permission of Alcoholics Anonymous World Services, Inc. (A.A.W.S.). Permission to reprint the Twelve Steps does not mean that Alcoholics Anonymous is in any way affiliated with this publication, or that it has read and/or endorses the contents thereof. A.A. is a program of recovery from alcoholism *only* — inclusion of the Steps in this publication, or use in any other non-A.A. context, does not imply otherwise. Additionally, while A.A. is a spiritual program, A.A. is not a religious program. Thus, A.A. is not affiliated or allied with any sect, denomination, or specific religious belief.

2. Came to believe that a Power greater than ourselves could restore us to sanity.

   "For by grace you have been saved through faith, and this is not your own doing; it is the gift of God — not the result of works, so that no one may boast." (Eph. 2:8–9)

3. Made a decision to turn our will and our lives over to the care of God, as we understood Him.

   "Come to me, all you that are weary and are carrying heavy burdens, and I will give you rest. Take my yoke upon you, and learn from me; for I am gentle and humble in heart, and you will find rest for your souls." (Matt. 11:28–29)

4. Made a searching and fearless moral inventory of ourselves.

   "Examine yourselves to see whether you are living in the faith." (2 Cor. 13:5)

5. Admitted to God, to ourselves and to another human being the exact nature of our wrongs.

   "The prayer of faith will save the sick, and the Lord will raise them up; and anyone who has committed sins will be forgiven. Therefore confess your sins to one another, and pray for one another, so that you may be healed." (James 5:15–16)

6. Were entirely ready to have God remove all these defects of character.

   "Now I rejoice, not because you were grieved, but because your grief led to repentance." (2 Cor. 7:9)

7. Humbly asked him to remove our shortcomings.

   "Humble yourselves before the Lord, and he will exalt you." (James 4:10)

8. Made a list of all persons we had harmed, and became willing to make amends to them all.

   "Do not judge, and you will not be judged; do not condemn, and you will not be condemned. Forgive and it will be forgiven; give and it will be given to you." (Luke 6:37–38)

9. Made direct amends to such people wherever possible, except when to do so would injure them or others.

"Blessed are the peacemakers, for they will be called children of God." (Matt. 5:9)

10. Continued to take personal inventory, and when we were wrong promptly admitted it.

"Watch and pray, lest you enter into temptation. The spirit truly is ready, but the flesh is weak." (Mark 14:38)

11. Sought through prayer and meditation to improve our conscious contact with God as we understood Him, praying only for knowledge of His will for us and the power to carry that out.

"Ask, and it will be given you; search, and you will find; knock, and the door will be opened for you. For everyone who searches finds, and for everyone who knocks, the door will be opened." (Matt. 7:7–8)

12. Having had a spiritual awakening as the result of these steps, we tried to carry this message to alcoholics, and to practice these principles in all our affairs.

"Go home to your friends, and tell them how much the Lord has done for you, and what mercy he has shown you."

(Mark 5:19)

It is not up to the caring minister to diagnose or treat the disease of alcoholism or other drug abuse. The above is for your information and a better understanding of this sickness. Only if the caring minister is comfortable with this illness would an assignment to deal with alcoholism be given. Even then it would most likely be for a family member who had requested spiritual guidance. Because there is so much denial and shame caused by this disease, it may never be recognized or admitted by your care receiver, nor is it appropriate for the caring minister to suggest that alcoholism the problem. We are commissioned only to walk with others on their journey, to be present with them in prayer, and to listen. We do not have the duty or the power to cure. Only God has that capacity.

If parishioners bring up the problem and need referrals, suggest that they speak to the caring ministry supervisor or pastor. Along with Alcoholics Anonymous, there is other help available and information regarding treatment can be found in the Yellow Pages of your phone book under Alcoholism Treatment and Information. Hopefully, the family members will be urged to attend Al-Anon, a program begun by Lois, Bill W.'s wife, for the friends and families of those suffering from alcoholism. This sickness encompasses all who are associated with the individual actually using the drug.

Perhaps it is now obvious to those reading this chapter that this author is a recovering alcoholic. By the grace of God I have celebrated twenty-three years of sobriety. In the depths of despair and destruction, I was given the help for which I haltingly asked. At that time I could not believe that God could grant me anything, so far away from God did I feel. Yet God was always there for me when I asked, then as now. Some of the times have been difficult and some good, but all have been challenging and exciting as I have been given the gift of a new life. I did not lose my family in the course of my drinking, but I did miss out on much of my children's growing up. Those are years that can never be recaptured.

None of us goes unscarred by the experience of alcoholism. Trust takes time to rebuild. We are always at risk, for alcohol is "cunning, baffling, and powerful." Many alcoholics cannot accept this wonderful gift of sobriety. Many cannot seem to hold on to it but fall back into the dreadful chasm of addiction from which they cannot escape. I am one of the very blessed, for somehow I knew that with God's help and the program of AA freedom from this bondage was possible. May I never forget.

I end this chapter with the Serenity Prayer, with which we begin each Alcoholics Anonymous meeting:

> God grant me the serenity
> To accept the things I cannot change
> The courage to change the things I can
> And the wisdom to know the difference.

ॐ *Chapter 12*

Specialized Ministries

Now there are varieties of gifts, but the same Spirit; and there are varieties of services, but the same Lord; and there are varieties of activities, but it is the same God who activates all of them in everyone. To each is given the manifestation of the Spirit for the common good. (1 Cor. 12:4–7)

We've covered the building blocks of pastoral care, which are appropriate for any ministry situation. There are, however, some dos and don'ts, some practical suggestions and sensitivities that are specific to particular situations. This chapter provides some additional guidelines for such specialized ministries. It is offered only as an overview of each area addressed. For those who wish to pursue a subject with more rigor, there are excellent books available, many of which are listed in the Bibliography. The following specialty areas are summarized for hospital visitation, suicide intervention, and ministry to the depressed.

Hospital Visitation

I received the call that Ginny had just suffered a heart attack and had been rushed to a nearby hospital. With my own heart beating rapidly, I sped on, praying all the way for this saintly older woman. When I arrived, she was in the Cardiac Intensive Care Unit. I identified myself to the nurse and asked to go in to see Ginny. The nurse refused, which surprised me since I was wearing my clerical collar. "Then may I just stand in the door so that Ginny can see that I'm here?" I asked. "Okay, okay, I guess you can go in for just a moment," she answered reluctantly. As I walked into the cubicle, Ginny looked up and her worried frown eased into a smile as she greeted me. "Oh, it's Sarah. Now I know I'll be all right." I knew she needed to see me to help deflate her fears and give her the assurance that her church was standing with her in prayer, care, and support. Her adult son was there also and obviously anxious and frightened. This gave me a chance to be with him at this critical time and provide for him a contact person for future reference. I was there only a few minutes and uttered a short heartfelt prayer. Mother and son were visibly changed. In this foreign environment a familiar face and more importantly a person of faith and love had entered onto the scene. Gratefully, Ginny recovered.

Healing and recovery are dependent on many cooperating factors. We cannot compartmentalize the body, soul, and spirit. They are intimately interconnected and affect each other dramatically. The pastoral caregiver has a definite role in the recovery process and therefore has the right to be a part of the team effort.

Hospitalization falls into the category of a crisis. Even when the hospitalization is planned and elected, it still represents a visit into the unknown and unfamiliar. I like to sum up the whole experience as one in which a person is "being done unto." Be aware that the person you are visiting may be experiencing some or all of the following:

- little or no control over procedures

- confusion and lack of information

- fear of the outcome

- concerns and worry about family, money, job, diminished physical capacity

- crisis of faith

- embarrassment over lack of privacy

The Role of the Caring Minister

Again the caring minister can fulfill a unique role of listening, of simply being present, and of focusing on feelings rather than solutions. The caring minister can be the person who imparts hope, who brings the spiritual dimension into the situation, and who offers a prayer with the person and/or family.

If a family member is in the room, you may find that you need to minister to both. If the visitor seems to have a need to talk, you might ask him or her to walk down the hall with you to give the person a chance to express concerns and feelings about the loved one.

Guidelines for Visitation

- Do call the hospital before visiting; people are discharged more rapidly nowadays.

- Do check at the nurses' station to ask if it is okay to see the patient; however, do not ask about diagnosis or details of treatment.

- Do knock on the door and identify yourself.

- Do keep visits shorter than a normal caring minister visit. Focus on their capacity and need to share — not your own.

- Do be aware and respectful of hospital routines, while asserting your right to be there and the value of your presence.

- Do not give medical advice or share your own "war stories." Instead, explore their feelings regarding their medical treatment.

- Do offer to leave if medical personnel enter the room.

- Do offer a prayer. Expression of faith feeds body, soul, and spirit.

- Do not visit if you are sick.

- Do not sit on the bed. Sit in a chair to be at eye level if possible.

- Do not wear strong cologne.

- Do not engage in conversation with the person in the next bed (as a rule).

- Do not talk about the patient in the third person when others are in the room. Family and friends tend to do so and also tend to answer questions even when directed to the patient. Firmly, but gently, make it clear that you want to hear what the patient has to say.

Much of this is plain common sense. We can observe hospital protocol and still claim the value of our own presence and ministry. It may just be the factor that determines the outcome in a crisis moment as was the case for Myrtle (whom we met above in chapter 9 on "Wisdom People").

When Myrtle suffered her first major stroke, her pastoral caregiver was out of town and didn't arrive at the hospital until the next day. She found Myrtle in a sorry state, unable to speak or move. The minister talked gently with her for a few minutes, stroked her brow, held her hand, and noticed that Myrtle was attempting to speak. Just then the doctor and a nurse entered the room and were shocked to see Myrtle moving her lips. Thus far she had not responded to any stimulus or medical personnel. The doctor enlisted the help of the caring minister as an "interpreter" to Myrtle, who would respond only to the caregiver's voice. Through her, the doctor prompted Myrtle to wiggle her fingers and toes and then lift them. Within fifteen minutes Myrtle was able to focus and connect with the other faces and begin to speak. It was the turning point in her crisis; from there on her course was recovery. This incident was dramatic, yet it demonstrated the necessity for familiar, loving, caring people in the healing process.

Suicide Intervention

Unlike other crises in which we are called after the critical event, a suicide threat is an occasion in which the minister can be a factor in the prevention of a crisis. In suicide intervention the minister takes a more direct and assertive approach with the person at the crossroads.

Many people who attempt suicide do not wish to die. They've simply run out of options or their circumstances and depression cloud the view of alternatives and potential solutions. A crisis occurs in which the result can go either way, and again it is a ripe opportunity for the caring minister to be on hand to explore new choices.

The majority of people who attempt suicide are neither irrational, psychotic, or emotionally disturbed. They are separated from their coping skills and are being swept up and paralyzed by feelings of fear, hopelessness, helplessness, exhaustion, loneliness, hurt, anger, failure, or abandonment. Suicide is considered a way to deal with the avalanche of feelings or the solution to a situation that appears to have reached an impasse. One elderly woman carefully planned her own death because she ran out of money. She didn't want to die; she just couldn't pay her rent for the following month. She came within a pulse beat of succeeding, but fortunately there was an intervention. In the ensuing weeks and months her caring minister not only provided love and nonjudgmental care but also investigated resources for which she was eligible and located lower cost housing. Once the situation was corrected the caregiver and care receiver shifted their focus to the relationship. The outcome was a new lease on life and a deeper faith in the God who did not leave her orphaned.

Suicide intervention may be a frightening prospect for many. We may feel ill equipped to deal with such a highly charged crisis and may feel, mistakenly, that it is only highly trained professionals who can react skillfully. I was involved in three suicide interventions many years before I entered the ordained ministry. As I look back on those incidents I am thankful that what I lacked as an expert was made up for by instincts and common sense. In my later formal training, I discovered that my responses as a lay person formed the basis of effective techniques.

Responses of the Caring Minister

First of all, do not act shocked or hysterical. Speak calmly and with authority; you are going to take charge of the situation if need be. Do not make remarks such as:

"Don't talk like that; it can't be that bad!"

"You know it's a sin; aren't you afraid of going to hell?"

"But life is a precious gift; life can be beautiful."

"I can't believe you are considering this; you have so much going for you."

Believe what they say; take it seriously and act accordingly.

Ask specific, direct questions. You need vital information at this point such as who, what, when, where, and how. Avoid the "why" question, which can lead down the trail of subjectivity, blaming, and generalizing. Combine the skills learned in chapter 6, "Compatibility Checking," and chapter 10, "Care during Crisis," to form your approach. Working in tandem they provide the strategy of getting the facts and taking action. For example:

CARE RECEIVER: "I called to let you know I'm at the end of my rope and I can't go on.

CARING MINISTER: "Are you saying you're planning to kill yourself?"

CARE RECEIVER: "Yes."

CARING MINISTER: "Where are you?"

CARE RECEIVER: "I'm at home."

CARING MINISTER: "Is anybody with you?"

CARE RECEIVER: "No, I'm alone."

CARING MINISTER: "How are you going to kill yourself?"

CARE RECEIVER: "I thought I might take a bottle of aspirin or I might gas myself in the garage." *Or another scenario:* "I have a loaded gun in my night stand." (*This response reflects a more specific plan using more lethal means.*)

CARING MINISTER: "What exactly happened today to prompt this decision?"

CARE RECEIVER: "I got fired. It wasn't enough that my wife left me two months ago. Now this."

CARING MINISTER: "That is awful. I can't imagine your pain, *but* I don't want you to do this."

CARE RECEIVER: "I don't believe in anything anymore.

CARING MINISTER: "No, but I do. Since you've shared this with me, I'd like to have the chance to help find a way through this."

CARE RECEIVER: "Well, maybe I can wait a few days."

CARING MINISTER: "Yes, let's agree that you won't take any action on this without letting me know first."

Another tactic is to talk about the consequences of a suicide.

"How do you think this will affect your children (parents, friends, even pets)?"

I found this to be the most effective deterrent. As my friends began to face the devastation their deaths would cause for those whom they loved, it opened the way to consider other possibilities. However, in one case I was hard pressed to come up with a person who meant much to the person threatening suicide. So I became that person. I assured her I would be deeply grieved if she died, and I invited her to call me anytime, day or night, if she came to that point again.

Another consequence worth pointing out is the possible failure of an attempt. Worse even than death is the prospect of the attempt backfiring and causing paralysis or disability. Even the most lethal of means have been known to fail and leave a person permanently handicapped.

Let the care receiver know how you feel about what or is about to do:

"I don't want you to do this; I care about you."

"I feel frightened by what you're saying, and I'll do anything I can to find another way."

"I'm going to see you through this. We need some time to talk and begin to figure things out."

Call in the assistance of others. Although you may be skilled and have common sense you don't need to deal with such a crisis alone. Let the person know you need help from others such as clergy or counselors:

"I want to help you, and I know Pastor Roberts can give us some good feedback."

If the care receiver proceeds with the plan to commit suicide, call whoever is appropriate: police, clergy, suicide prevention experts.

Confidentiality need not be honored in cases of homicide, suicide, or child abuse. However, the care receiver must be informed of your intentions (unless there is a threat to your own life):

"Since I can't dissuade you, I will have to call _____."

In most cases, people call a pastor or a friend because they are searching for a ray of hope and a means to go forward. The call is a definite sign that they want and are open to help.

A Judeo-Christian View

Deliberate suicide needs to be distinguished from the willing surrender of one's life for defense of country, cause, or faith. In the latter cases one does not primarily will or choose one's own death, but is prepared for its possibility in an act of self-sacrifice.

Except for the explicit prohibition in the Ten Commandments "You shall not murder" (Exod. 20:13), there is a notable absence of commentary in the Bible on the issue of suicide. It is reported but not directly condemned. Later tradition labeled it a grave sin and went so far as to deny the rite of Christian burial to those who were guilty of "laying violent hands" upon themselves.

In this century suicide is understood in its many complex causes and states of mind. But it will probably always be a source of stigma for the suicidal and their families. The church's approach has shifted to one of compassion and understanding. In the hierarchy of "sins" it may have slipped a few pegs and taken its place among many other offenses that deny God's activity of grace. Our bodies and lives are entrusted to us by God, but suicide is not the only distortion that severs that stewardship and denies the faith community of mutual ministry, love, and support.

Suicide is, however, unique among the causes of death because of the enormous regret of those left behind. Sudden accidents leave the grieving with years of "what ifs," but suicide adds to those questions the haunting awareness that it might have been prevented. Would one more day have shed the light or provided the strength to overcome the obstacle or the paralyzing emotional pain?

The Christian is well equipped to bargain for those days needed to impart hope. Love is not only stronger than death; it is also stronger than despair, pain, or any crisis.

Ministry to the Depressed

Almost any loss is going to trigger, to some degree, the sinking feeling of depression. Even seemingly small losses can cause a momentary wave of sadness and an altered outlook. Deeper states of depression will normally be manifested in the aftermath of a life-changing crisis. It's as if one awakens from a bad dream only to discover that the nightmare is real. After the shock and numbness wear off the full impact of events stare a person squarely in the eye. Depression affects the whole person, body, mind, and spirit, and healing will come about by addressing all these aspects through a collaboration of resources.

Caring ministers, and clergy for that matter, are no substitutes for counselors and medical professionals, but we can be crucial instruments of support and hope. For our purposes we'll be examining depression as it relates to a specific crisis or acute situation. It is inappropriate for a lay minister to be the sole support person for anyone with chronic emotional disorders or long-term clinical depression. However, there might be occasions for pastoral caregivers to be included in the network of someone under the care of physicians and therapists.

Although we are not counselors, we should become well acquainted with the characteristic signs and symptoms of depression. This enables us to be alert to the need to refer or to enlist other resources, and it helps us situate our own faithful response within the total healing process. We have an authority and a faith tradition that offer a unique perspective on the healing of persons.

What Is Depression?

The causes of depression are those identified in chapter 7, "Understanding Loss, Grief, and Death." Depression can be one among many emotions we feel when undergoing a crisis or transition. But it can also take over a person's ability to cope. It claims a life of its own with its own additional list of descriptives and symptoms:

inactivity	loss of appetite
reclusiveness	irritability
lack of energy	physical and mental sluggishness
cloak of sadness on the face	difficulty in concentrating
feelings of utter loneliness	getting too much or too little sleep
negativity about the future:	negative self-talk:
"It will never be any different."	"I'm worthless."

Ask any group of people to brainstorm about depression, and you might hear some of these responses:

alone	black hole	suffocating	aridity
no energy	hopeless	anguish	vast emptiness
lost	gloominess	darkness	sinking in quicksand

You will have additions, no doubt, since depression seems to be an experience common to everyone. One or two symptoms alone do not paralyze a person's ability to effect change. But if many of these symptoms and feelings are manifested in the care receiver, they indicate that normal grief and sadness remain unresolved and have been prolonged into a depression.

Spiritual Light in the Darkness

So many of the words in the list above are descriptive of the landscape in a desert. We can turn this to our advantage by connecting the experience of depression with one of the most powerful metaphors of the Judeo-Christian tradition: the wilderness or desert journey.

People who are depressed seem to be camped out in desolate, unfriendly territory. It is an in-between stop-off where choices need to be made for either life or death. The danger of death lurks when the destination of the promised land is all but forgotten, and they look backward to a life that no longer exists.

Many people slip into this state when they hold on to methods of operation that have become obsolete. They are attempting to behave exactly as they did prior to the crisis or change in circumstances, and it simply doesn't work. Longing for what used to be becomes a form of idolatry as well as an unproductive path.

For example: Jim was an elderly man who could not properly grieve or adjust to the change in his role or the diminishment of his health. Eventually he became an invalid confined to a wheelchair and unable to handle home and fiscal affairs. He flatly refused to give his family any access to his financial information. He purchased a new car, which he could not drive, and acquired two cats, which were not permitted in his retirement complex. Not surprisingly, this led to even deeper depression as the car and the cats became tangible reminders of his failing health. Eventually, his family was forced to intervene, and Jim found himself with even less independence than before. Jim wanted everything to be the way it used to be, but life seldom works out that way.

A woman can often experience the same dynamic when the nest empties and her young adult children begin to relate as adult, to adult but she persists in maintaining an adult-child relationship. The "empty" in "empty nest" becomes an apt description as she is challenged to discover a new role and identity for herself. An alternative response to her resistance is expressed in the metaphor of "new wineskins for new wine." The old wineskins, or the obsolete ways of operating, need to be discarded, or the results are all too predictable.

In our desert analogy the wilderness provided the perfect environment for transformation. Bereft of former attachments and loss of former caretakers, the Hebrews were left to look deeply into their own identity and discover their relationship to God. The theme of the desert has historically been applied to the spiritual journey and may further help us claim the redemptive dimension of depression.

There are few, if any, Christians on a serious disciplined path with God who have not spent a season in the desert. It is described as spiritual aridity, dryness, lack of feeling in prayer, and wondering if God is there. When my own directees share such symptoms with me, I can scarcely keep my enthusiasm in low gear. I know that God is urging them to a new level of maturity and an unfolding of who God is in truth rather than who they currently fashion God to be. The emptiness and aridity wean the pilgrim from comfortable and familiar routines, which may have become spiritual idols in themselves. It is a place for the obsolete to wither and die and for the pilgrim to remain alive and to proceed forward. The key is to go through the desert; going around only lengthens the journey, and turning back is slavery to immaturity. The path through is by way of faithfulness to the encounter with God. It includes an honest dialogue, a listening for the new Word to be revealed. God may reveal just a subtle facet or disclose only a nuance of love. But those small unveilings become the occasions of rejoicing and thankfulness for director and directee in much the same way as King David stopped, worshiped, and danced before the Lord after the Ark of the Covenant had been moved only six paces (2 Sam. 6:13–14).

In order for the Israelites to navigate the wilderness they needed their own "spiritual director" in the person of Moses. Likewise the depressed person requires the presence of at least one who will fulfill the key role of prophet. Pastoral caregivers can exercise this call in much the same way as Moses did.

The Prophet Keeps the Destination Alive

Moses was responsible for keeping the vision of the promised land always before his people. Depressed people need to be reminded that there is a future, that there is a life beyond the present circumstances, that there is a goal of wholeness and well-being. This hope is not achieved with hollow assurances, but with thoughtful reflection on the past and realistic exploration of future options. There are times when the caring minister can exude genuine confidence that things will get better. In the case of the woman who attempted suicide because she could not pay the rent, her caregiver knew there were available resources and she set the wheels in motion. Her reassurances were rooted in reality, not wishful thinking. Another applicable image is that of the midwife who holds the hand and wipes the brow of the woman giving birth. Soothing words of encouragement are given along the way with the reminder of the new life emerging.

The Prophet Is the Reminder of God's Faithfulness

"Remember how God brought you up out of the land of Egypt? . . . Remember the crossing of the Red Sea? Remember the manna that fell from the heavens? Remember?" Their rehearsal of God's unfailing activity formed the basis of the Israelites unity as a people and of their liturgical worship. Lest we chide them for their short attention span, we need only remind ourselves that we are still sharing the very same story of freedom from the exile of sin. Our faith is nurtured by the same old story of redemption in our celebration of the Paschal mystery. Caring ministers gently probe the graced moments of the past when God's presence could be felt.

The Prophet Is the Great Organizer

As Moses kept the destination alive, he also had to face the practical necessity of day-to-day living. There was much to be done in the wilderness. People had to eat and sleep and work, and Moses provided the leadership to help organize them into a community. Sometimes through simple listening the caregiver makes that happen. As the care receivers verbalize all that is going on, they can see new paths and directions and begin to effect some orderliness. There are also those times when the caring minister needs to be a true shepherd and adopt a more directive role. Since the depressed experience low energy and activity levels they need a gentle nudge to take the first step. For example: "I'm going to ask you to get out of bed, shower, and get dressed tomorrow, even if that's all you do." Activity helps break the negative patterns set during depression. These small steps can make hope real in the present tense and ignite further motivation.

The Prophet Animates the Dialogue

The Israelites cannot be accused of being timid about complaining to Moses about their fear, loss, anger, hurt, and confusion. Moses did not always like what he was hearing, but he listened and conveyed the complaints to God. The dialogue between the people, Moses, and God throughout forty years was a vital piece in forming their identity. Such formation cannot take place in a monologue. Depressed people who have no supportive listener are left to repeat their negative self-talk ad nauseam, but enter the caring minister who listens and dialogues and an environment is created for new insights.

This was illustrated to me through the experience of Catherine. I was departing for the summer and felt the need to visit her before I left, assuming it would be the last time I would see her since she was suffering from heart disease, osteoporosis, Parkinson's, and chronic depression. When I arrived her nurse aide took me aside and informed me that Catherine was talking about her desire to die. Her family members were upset by this and resisted her attempts to verbalize what she was feeling. Her comments were met with, "Oh, don't talk like that; you're not dying." "We still need you; you're going to be okay." When the bedridden Catherine began to pour out her heart, I held her hand and listened. She was ready to die. The pain and the day-to-day struggle were too much for her, and she felt like a burden to her overtaxed family. She expressed no fears about dying, sounded at peace, and asked me if I thought she was wrong in wanting to give up. I reflected back to her all she had shared and added that this was her journey and if she felt ready she could offer it up to God and release herself to the Lord's good intentions. She seemed surprised by the whole conversation. When we bid our "goodbyes," I did not expect to see her again.

I returned to work three months later, and Catherine was still alive. I made an appointment with her, anxious to see in what state I would find her. She greeted me with a pitcher of Bloody Marys and a bowl of mixed nuts. She declared, "This is to celebrate that I lived through the summer." "Catherine, you look so much better. What happened?" I asked. She answered, "You scared me when you said I could die if I wanted to. After you left, I began to think that I didn't really want to die, and so I got better."

I didn't actually scare Catherine; her own words jolted her. Our dialogue enabled her to reach down very deeply to her core desires. Although she had voiced her sentiments to her family, they remained a monologue as long as no one would listen. Dialogue requires a two-way interaction in order to get below surface clichés. Caring ministers carry the mirror of reflective listening that can jolt, inspire, and encourage the care receivers to tap their own resources.

The Prophet Provides a Structure

Measured by the standards of surrounding cultures, especially that of the Egyptians, the Israelites were an unsophisticated and under-developed people. Yet, they were chosen to receive one of the most revolutionary structures for living the world has ever seen: the Law. It was a key for living in harmony: "You'll be happier if you don't murder, steal, covet, etc." It unveiled the relationship with God as the primary underlying focus of life. The Law was given to maintain and nurture community stability and communion with the divine originator. The Mosaic Law formed the identity of the Hebrews more than anything else. It gave them direction, it transformed them; they needed its structure to go forward and leave the desert behind. The Law provided the framework for the revelation of the Covenant and the principle of divine/human interaction. The substance beneath the structure was the God who longed to be united to the beloved Israel. Nevertheless, the structure of the Law could become a sub-stitute for the substance. To prevent such idolatry, any framework needs to be examined for its ability to ignite the fires of faith.

The caregiver can create a structure with depressed people by looking at healthy ways for them to experience healing in body, mind, and spirit. The framework might be described as an action plan. It moves beyond the inward gaze of the depressed and chal-lenges them to situate their lives in relation to work, family, friends, physical health. Together the caring minister and the care receiver re-view what is working and what is not working. It's the view of the big picture and the harmonies that open up new directions.

The Prophet Connects with the Covenant

The Hebrews were much more than a few tribes attempting to es-cape their oppressors and claim their own land and autonomy. They were children of the promise, chosen by a God driven to lavish love upon them and to be their ever-present sustainer. Whenever they be-came disconnected from their source of meaning, Moses was there to remind them and to intercede. In cultivating his own intimacy with the Holy, Moses was able to be authentic in his leadership;

it sprang from a divine/human collaboration that honed his skills *and* depended on God to accomplish the change of heart.

Spiritual Application

After you become engaged in ministry with a care receiver, you might use the following exercise as a means to examine and reflect upon your prophetic role.

- **Keep the Destination Alive**
  Have you been able to impart hope without false optimism?
  What do you see in this person's future that gives rise to hope?
  What "destination" is realistic?

- **Be the Reminder of God's Faithfulness**
  Can the care receiver name other times in his or her life when God's sustaining grace was evident? A revisit to those times can activate a rich theological reflection that may even offer understanding of the current experience.

- **Promote the Care Receiver's Organizational Ability**
  Can you identify obvious small steps that the care receiver can take to help support habits of healing? These are the little choices people make that help to break depressive behaviors.

- **Maintain the Dialogical Nature of the Relationship**
  Are your conversations monologues (by either of you) or dialogues of mutual communication?

  If you are doing too much talking, what is your motive? Are you in a fix-it mode? How does your care receiver respond to your monologue? What might you do or say to shift to dialogue?

  If the care receiver who is stuck in a monologue with seemingly no interest in mutual sharing, ask yourself, "Does he or she still need to rehearse the crisis event until it becomes real or is it time to move beyond information to reflection and response?"

- **Reinforce Healthy Structures**
  What patterns for coping has the care receiver created that are positive? Are there any that are negative?

- **Connect with the Covenant**

  How is the care receiver able to connect this experience with God's good intention for his or her life?

  In your devotional life how are you cultivating intimacy with God, thus nurturing your own authentic pastoral care identity?

Pastoral care by those who take seriously their own need for encounter with God brings a special gift to the relationship. They need to go to the mountain of prayer when the care receivers are too fearful or confused to utter anything other than "take away my pain and make me feel better." The caring minister believes, hopes, intercedes, and calls upon the God of promise for meaning and the deepening of faith. The prophetic ministry of the caregiver can mean the difference between unredeemed suffering and bringing the experience into the circle and service of God's love.

∾ *Chapter 13*

The First Caring Visit

Then an angel of the Lord said to Philip, "Get up and go to-
ward the south to the road that goes down from Jerusalem to
Gaza." . . . So he got up and went. Now there was an Ethiopian
eunuch, a court official of Candace, queen of the Ethiopians, in
charge of her entire treasury. He had come to Jerusalem to wor-
ship and was returning home; seated in his chariot, he was reading
the prophet Isaiah. Then the Spirit said to Philip, "Go over to this
chariot and join it." So Philip ran up to it and heard him read-
ing from the prophet Isaiah. He asked, "Do you understand what
you are reading?" He replied, "How can I, unless someone guides
me?" And he invited Philip to get in and sit beside him. . . . The eu-
nuch asked Philip, "About whom, may I ask you, does the prophet
say this, about himself or about someone else?" Then Philip began
to speak, and starting with this scripture, he proclaimed to him the
good news about Jesus. (Acts 8:26–31, 34–35)

You have studied, read, learned, shared, and prayed, and now the
day has come for which you have prepared. You knock on the
door not knowing what awaits you in the next hour. Suddenly you
feel nervous, exposed, and alone. Everything you thought you knew
seems to be going up in smoke. Good for you! You happen to be
perfectly normal and you are demonstrating the very posture necessary to leave you free to be equipped for ministry. If you have been
faithful to the reading, prayer, formation, and critical reflection pre-
sented in this book, you are ready. In the final phase of preparation,
a review of some meaningful skills and the characteristics of a first
interview is necessary.

Using the above passage from Acts as a model visit, let us
highlight significant moments that influenced its positive outcome.

An angel of the Lord said to Philip, "Get up and go...."

The very foundation of our service and ministry is the call from God. Our energy and empowerment are rooted in the acknowledgment of this collaboration. God directed; Philip responded.

So Philip ran up to the chariot and heard him reading from the prophet Isaiah.

Philip began the pastoral care relationship by *listening* and *noticing* what the Ethiopian was reading. Philip focused on the other's frame of reference, not his own.

He asked, "Do you understand what you are reading?"

Philip indicated his interest by asking good questions that were in context.

He replied, "How can I, unless someone guides me?" And he invited Philip to get in and sit beside him.

A peer relationship began that would not have happened if Philip had approached him with a superior attitude. They sat side by side, eye to eye, and listened together for the Word to be revealed.

Then Philip began to speak, and starting with the scripture, he proclaimed to him the good news about Jesus.

It was only after Philip listened, was invited, sat as a peer, and entered into a thoughtful dialogue that he presumed to speak. Even in his response to the Ethiopian he remained faithful to the context of the dialogue. The fruit of Philip's servant ministry was the *naming* of this man's deep longing: Jesus. Caring ministers are the catalysts who help people label and summon their own resources and who discover with them access to divine initiative.

The Initial Telephone Call

Understandably you will probably be nervous the first time you call your care receiver and the first time you meet. Performers, clergy, and people who do public speaking find themselves buoyed up and energized by a slight nervousness. In ministry it prompts a humble, open attitude. You have learned in your training the building blocks of listening, focusing on feelings, and crisis intervention. These will now serve you as you combine them with your own desire to care for those who are hurting. The most important thing to remember and to claim is that you do not go alone. Christ is not just your companion, but goes before you in compassion and love.

With regard to the initial telephone call:

- The care receiver will always be prepared for your call by one of the other parish staff.

- Identify yourself as being from the church and use the name of the clergy person or lay pastoral person who referred you: "This is Mary Smith from St. John's. Fr. Frank tells me you are recovering from back surgery and that you would appreciate a visit. When would be a good time for me to stop by?" Do not say, "Would you like me to visit you?" The care receiver has already requested a visitor, and asking the question in this way requires the person to ask for help again.

- The first telephone call will generally not be a good time to go into depth about the care receiver's concerns or problems. Try to save that for the first face-to-face visit.

The First Visit

After you have set up the appointment and before your first meeting you may find yourself more at ease by (1) reading this chapter and chapter 3, on listening, and (2) spending some time in prayer. The reading is a review of information while the prayer creates a disposition of trust and spiritual fortification. Both are needed on this all-important visit. Here are some other pointers:

Be on time. Not only is this a simple matter of courtesy, but tardiness can produce anxiety in the care receiver. Is she coming? Did she forget? Does she really want to see me? This anxiety is especially exaggerated for shut-ins and frail elderly. The ticking of the clock seems much slower when a person is waiting and lonely.

Be yourself. God has called you for a particular reason. There is something about you that God needs in the divine/human collaboration. People can see through any attempts to be someone you are not. You may be nervous, but chances are the care receiver will not even notice. He or she is wrapped up in personal need and is not concerned with how you are performing. Once you start listening and focusing on the story, your nervousness will disappear.

Keep small talk to a minimum. You are there for a purpose. If you engage too long in chit-chat it will be awkward to approach the subject matter. Get to the point. For example:

> "Fr. Frank explained to me that your divorce became final last week. Would you tell me a little more about it?"

In case of an elderly shut-in who is not experiencing an acute loss but the slow, chronic losses of aging, a more appropriate lead-in statement might be:

> "Pastor Connie tells me that you've been a member of St. Mark's for over sixty years. I'd be interested to know what it was like over the years," *or*

> "I understand you moved into this facility a few months ago. It must be quite a transition for you.

Use the first visit for information gathering. You need to put the picture together. It will be natural to explore the who, what, when, where, and how of the situation. This is the first visit of many, and it may not be until later that critical reflection and effective dialogue take place. This is the time to establish rapport, get the facts of the story, and break the ice. Remember our comparison to *lectio divina*. The first step is to "Read" and get acquainted with the Scripture. This first pastoral care visit is the first "Read" of the person and the precipitating event.

Establish the norm of confidentiality. Sometime during the initial sharing, make it clear that everything will be kept confidential. Pastoral care is a sacred trust with no difference in professional ethics between lay and clergy. The name of the care receiver should not be identified even to other caring ministers. The only exceptions are conversations with the pastoral care supervisor who made the assignment or discussions in a general mutual ministry support group where the name of the care receiver is changed. Beyond professional ethics, common sense dictates the necessity of confidentiality. The pastoral caregiver *never* discloses the identity of the care receiver and never discusses the person with family, or friends no matter how well intentioned.

Establish the norm of assertive behavior. Communicate clearly your own limitations and boundaries as the need arises:

CARE RECEIVER: "I wonder if you could take me to the doctor on Friday. I've had to give up driving."

CARING MINISTER: "I work weekdays and am unable to do that. I believe the Red Cross offers a transportation service for seniors. If you'd like we could look up the number now."

Saying no does not require long explanations nor any apologies. Short, direct "I" statements are both clear and comfortable. We've talked about the respect we bring to the caring relationship, and it includes respect for ourselves. Assertiveness is a communication tool that affirms our need and our right to make free choices. Being assertive involves taking responsibility for our own actions and feelings. Saying no doesn't mean we don't care but demonstrates we have developed a certain wisdom about ourselves. Effective caring ministers do not allow themselves to become consumed in doing pastoral care. Again we look to Jesus as an example who took care of his own needs and honored his own desires and his call to spend time alone in prayer, to relax at special occasions and dinners, and to go fishing with his good friends. In the Gospel record of his life there is no indication that he ever allowed guilt or the manipulation of others to rule his course. He managed to be responsible and compassionate while maintaining a positive level of self-respect and care.

Take the initiative for closing the visit. Be alert to any signals from the care receiver that it is time to go. Or if your agreed upon time is coming to a close, approach the need to end with simple, direct statements.

"I think we are at a good stopping place. Do you have anything to add before I leave?" *or*

"Our time is almost up and I need to go. Do you feel comfortable about stopping here?"

Avoid closing statements that put the blame on the care receiver.

"You look tired. I think I've worn you out. I'd better let you go."

If the care receiver introduces a subject that requires a whole new exploration, be clear about your need and intention to end:

"Your dad's interference in this opens up a whole new area to consider. Let's begin next week's meeting by looking at it."

If the care receiver persists in trying to extend the visit, be assertive in your response:

"I need to leave now, and I can't give this new issue the attention it deserves. I'll make a note to pick up our conversation here next time we meet."

You may also want to summarize the visit or make a concluding remark:

"I feel very moved by your story and complicated circumstances. I see a great deal of strength coming forth in you, and I'd like to support you along the way."

Set up the next meeting before you leave. This will save time in the long run and will affirm your intent to continue the caring relationship. Remember, you are the initiator of the relationship. It is part of the caregiver's outreach of compassion to assume responsibility for setting up meetings. In most cases it is inadvisable to leave it to the care receiver to initiate future appointments.

Be prepared to close with a prayer. This is the greatest source of nervousness and anxiety for caring ministers. Not only do many feel awkward about praying aloud, they are also unsure about the care receiver's openness to discussing the spiritual dimension of their lives. The wisest approach is to arrive with something in hand that is suitable and familiar to your own faith tradition, such as a prayer or psalm from the Book of Common Prayer. If you feel comfortable praying spontaneously, form your prayer out of the context of your dialogue and sharing. There is the great, universally familiar Lord's Prayer, which seems always able to collect people's yearnings and feelings into one beautiful expression. Again, be simple and direct, asking the care receiver at the close of the visit if he or she would like a prayer. If the offer is declined, that's fine; make it again the next time. Prayer has a way of bonding people very tenderly, and it can also release some deep wellsprings of emotion and spiritual sensitivity.

Take time alone to reflect on the visit. Review the conversation and consider these questions:

- What information did I hear?

- What feelings did I identify?

- What feelings may be hidden?

- What is the care receiver's greatest strength? greatest weakness?

- What are my own feelings about the interview?

- Did the dialogue remind me of any painful events in my life?

Finally, pray for yourself and for your care receiver. Imagine the two of you sitting in the chariot side by side listening together to the Word of God. If you practice Centering Prayer, let go of all thoughts, emotions, and imagery, take your care receiver with you into the silence, and rest all your cares in God's love.

Conclusion

The initial visit is the first of many to come. It is not necessary to cover everything at once; that is not the purpose of the caring ministry. Healing is a process that requires its own time frame for sowing, for nurturing, and for bearing fruit.

Finally, here is Robert Francisco's reflection on his relationship with his first care receiver.

LaHoma Stewart, My First Care Receiver

I can still remember going out on my first visit as a lay eucharistic minister to see LaHoma. She sat waiting patiently through my awkward set-up for Communion. I was particularly nervous, knowing that she had served on the Altar Guild and knew everything about setting up for Communion.

Through the four years that followed, a relationship evolved. Sometimes I would just read from the Book of Common Prayer. She would enjoy hearing the Rite I Eucharistic Prayer. I would tell her about a retreat, a new priest, a guest clergy person, who read the Gospel, or what happened in church school.

I could tell she was always listening intently. As much as she suffered, sometimes just waiting for someone to bring her a cool drink, she was always eager to hear someone else's story rather than being consumed by her own misery.

LaHoma's meal schedule often coincided with my visits. Often I would arrive to find her sitting at the restorative feeding table waiting for help. She allowed me the privilege of feeding her small portions of peas, carrots, meat, and potatoes. I felt it was appropriate to help her with bodily nourishment before giving her Communion. We were both fed by the shared experience.

One Sunday I brought a close friend of mine, Michelle, to church. She was visiting from Oregon. It was Kirkin' o' the Tartan, a large, impressive service. She viewed organized religion with suspicion and decided not to take Communion.

After the service, Michelle accompanied me as I brought Communion to LaHoma. During the short presentation of Communion, Michelle read John 20:19–31 — the resurrected Christ appears to his disciples, and doubting Thomas comes to believe.

The Gospel reading and the whole experience with LaHoma touched Michelle, and she and her close friend, Roxanne, joined the Methodist Church the following year. They went on to touch the lives of many people.

LaHoma's capacity to witness was never diminished by the ravages of Parkinson's disease or her isolation. I believe Michelle's reading of the Gospel while visiting LaHoma allowed a transformation to take place through the work of the Holy Spirit.

We too, in our own desolate experiences perhaps yet to come, can provide valuable witness to those who may come our way. Through my visits with LaHoma, I learned what it means to overcome death as we shared and were nurtured in our spiritual journeys.

Spiritual Application

My soul proclaims your greatness, O God, and my spirit rejoices in you, my Savior.   (Luke 1:47 Inclusive New Testament)

We have used the following prayer, "The Body Prayer," to begin many of our group process sessions, and people have adopted it for personal prayer as well. It is excellent as a waking prayer or as the benediction at the close of the day since it joins body and spirit in one act of releasing all to God.

Stand with your feet together and your body at gentle attention, head tall and hands with palms facing at the heart position (as in prayer). Inhale as you bring your arms up and over your head, palms still facing. Reach high and stretch as you inhale. Now turn your hands and place them back to back. Bring them down to your sides as you exhale. (These movements are done with good stretching and strong breathing.)

As you lift your arms the first time, lift all the concerns of your life to God. As you turn your palms over, release them to God. (Repeat three times.)

Next, as you lift your arms, lift all the people in your life to God: family, friends, and your care receiver. (Repeat three times.)

Finally, lift yourself, your life work, and your ministry to God. (Repeat three times.)*

---

*Mardi Erdman was a beloved Christian yoga teacher in Denver, Colorado, who died of cancer at the age of fifty-six in the Spring of 1994. This Body Prayer was given to her while in meditation and she offered it to students throughout the world. Her husband responded when we asked to use the prayer in caring ministry training, "This was her gift."

Meditation on Suffering

Do not be ashamed, then, of the testimony about our Lord or of me his prisoner, but join with me in suffering for the gospel, relying on the power of God, who saved us and called us with a holy calling, not according to our works but according to his own purpose and grace. This grace was given to us in Christ Jesus before the ages began. (2 Tim. 1:8–9)

Our call to minister, to love, to care, takes us inevitably to those who suffer. In them and in our own aches we encounter one of the principal themes of our faith. It seems at times that much is asked of Christians. The belief in God's spectacular interventions and miracles challenges our reason. Falling manna, feeding of thousands, raising the dead, healing the demented, virgin birth, and resurrection have all become subjects of scholarship and debate. But they seldom become the daily battlefield on which faith is fought in quite the same way as suffering. It is the daily companion of countless souls who yearn to find meaning and solace in their experience.

Gratefully, we have long since shed the belief that suffering is a judgment for sin. The lessons from Job and Jesus clarified that for all time. We have learned to assign much of suffering to its authentic sources:

- foolish indulgences (smoking, overeating, self-destructive choices)

- the human condition (disease, free will, imperfections of body and soul)

- accidents (we simply bump into each other)

- the laws of nature (we are a part of nature and subject to, for example, gravity, earthquakes, volcanos, droughts, etc.)

- the mystery of evil and its devices

We could list countless examples of tragedy under each heading and bemoan the state of the world. The Christian is called to live with the assumption that none of these sources of suffering extends beyond the reach of God's enfolding love. Not even evil, as heinous and powerful as it may manifest itself, is outside of God's capacity to imbue the worst events with resurrection power. God can embrace all catastrophes in divine providence. The Spirit summons us beyond ourselves, beyond our limited horizon and resources, and proposes new insights into God's self-disclosure.

If suffering is our unwelcome companion, Jesus is the way to discover God's healing action along the way. Jesus is not the revealer of the path. He *is* the path and the ground that provides stability in chaos. He gets us through the point of crisis by connecting our desire for order and wholeness to our most seminal desire for meaning and transcendence.

Have you ever wondered why Jesus never explained evil and suffering? Except for the hint of the query in John 9:2 — "...who sinned, this man or his parents, that he should be born blind?" — it appears no one asked. Suffering was part of the fabric of life and, for the most part, out of the sphere of control of most people. We, on the other hand, have learned to exercise control over much of our surroundings. We don't need to tread a dusty trail from Galilee to Jerusalem. We can e-mail our messages. Science has cured smallpox, polio, bacterial infections, and many cancers. We get what we want when we want it at the flip of a switch or the turn of a knob. But we are brought up short and reminded of just how little we can control when we are shaken by an earthquake or buried in a hundred-year blizzard. We can land a mini-rover successfully on Mars but feel helpless and foolish days later when it gets stuck against a rock. The illusion of power under which we operate only serves to heighten our reaction of devastation when our plans go awry. Our anger and frustration build to a climax of blaming God and begging the question: "Why?"

The question "Why?" is accompanied by an accusation or a judgment and is usually followed by "...and why didn't you do otherwise?" Jesus managed to escape the ultimate "Why?" question; perhaps he knew the futility of such a project. He refrained from becoming the philosopher and dealt with the human condition as the quintessential pastor who plowed through suffering rather than wading in its mire. We return to the teaching of earlier chapters: don't ask "why?"; ask "who, what, when, where, and how?"

The principle of Jesus' pastoral response and ours is to *confront* and *confound* the chaos, suffering, and evil we meet. Jesus did not explain evil; he confronted it with love. He encountered people in their concrete struggle and explored with them the who, what, when, where, and how: "Who will feed them?" "Where is your treasure?" "What does it profit?" He invited people first to see their own experience and to describe it; this in itself can be very prickly. But the next step of peeling off the layers was necessary to unveil the true nature of chaos and authentic desire for meaning. The lengthy dialogue with the Samaritan woman is a perfect case. She is transformed from context to contemplation. She begins with, "I'm tired of the drudgery of getting water everyday," which leads to, "I'm sick of being used by men," which unfolds to, "What I want most of all is to be loved and known for who I am in my deepest self." We cannot begin with meaning and transcendence. They are the fruit of a faithful process that begins with the confrontation of current circumstances.

The glimpse of the Samaritan woman reminds us of another of the famous attributes of Jesus' ministry. He did not conform to opinion, culture, or the conventional wisdom of his day. What motivated him was his complete compatibility with his own mission to do the will of God. He managed, with great style, to avoid the temptation of reacting to his environment and instead proceeded in accordance with his deepest self and call. He was not seduced by popularity. When the reviews were great and the crowds were swelling, he would often disappear for prayer. He didn't assume a panic posture even when those around him did. Mary and Martha sent for him (John 11:3) but he lingered; he was warned of Herod's threat (Luke 13:31–32), but he didn't flee. We could say he remained centered, knowing just when to come and when to go, when to speak and when to pray, when to live and when to die. Likewise, the prayerfully centered caring minister remains steady, does not rush into premature actions, yet proceeds with a style that confronts the real and, at the same time, nurtures the hurting.

∽✺✥∾

Jesus confronted suffering and evil with love. In so doing he confounded evil and derailed it from its purpose. Evil expects us to react to trouble and crisis by cursing God, retaliating, yielding to despair, and giving in to the feeling of being crushed, forsaken, and destroyed (2 Cor. 4:8–9). Evil expects us to treat our enemies, even the enemies within, with hatred. Evil rejoiced when Judas hung himself. Whenever our antiphon to affliction is love, evil loses its hold.

Love is ultimately our only advantage over chaos. It is the way to confuse it, disarm it, and diminish its power. The cross and resurrection stand out as great acts of disarming love. The resurrection is the greatest protest song ever written against injustice and violence, and we are privileged to carry the spirit of the resurrection within us.

The caregiver who is there in the face of the blackest despair and who acknowledges its pain but sticks with it is consenting to resurrection power and steadfast love.

The difficult pill to swallow in all of this is the realization that we cannot "fix it." If we could, we would. We would seize the power to rewind life and to change the traumatizing circumstances. However, we can only view the instant replay and relive the experience over and over again with every nuance of feeling.

But why should we expect to "fix it" when that is not even God's role? God is not the great problem solver of the universe but the great lover of the universe. Oh, yes, God is active. God's loving activity, urges, woos, pushes, and draws humankind to move forward in the "kind intention of God's will" (Eph. 1:5). God's invitation to us is joint participation in the divine project of supplanting evil with the substantive Christ form of love.

Although Jesus in fact healed people, fed great crowds, and even raised people from the dead on a couple of occasions, such events did not form the bedrock of his ministry. He was only an occasional problem solver whose chief purpose was to pour out God's love upon us (Rom. 5:5), regenerate us (John 3:5–6), teach us (John 14:26), disclose the truth (John 16:13), abide in us (John 14:16–

17), and produce Christ's fruits in us (Gal. 5:22–23). The emphasis is on encounter. I am not suggesting that God is not interested in our everyday troubles, and I hope we have all experienced what we might label as divine interventions. These do not occur every day and should not, lest we miss out on the cultivation of God's surpassing gift: divine union. Supernatural interruptions do not shape us into mature Christians. Mature interaction, born out of the day-to-day cultivation of knowledge of God through prayer, worship, Scripture reading, and community, creates the holy ground of transformation and providence. Jesus revealed the divine overture of lavish love.

Who other than Jesus can shed divine light on our struggle with suffering? St. Peter wrote about it with relish but it was St. Paul who sounded positively giddy over his persecutions, shipwrecks, imprisonments, and beatings. In examining one of his superlative statements on the subject, in 2 Timothy 1:8–12, we can indeed uncover the source of his confounding joy:

> *...join with me in suffering for the Gospel...*

St. Paul knew clearly the focus of his life, his call, and his deepest identity in God. More than a cause, the Gospel was his being.

> *...relying on the power of God...*

With all of Paul's credentials, gifts, talents, and knowledge, he discovered the power beyond human competency.

> *...who saved us and called us, not according to our works but according to his own purpose and grace. This grace was given to us in Christ Jesus before the ages began...*

Paul is now swept into the contemplative dimension. He yields his own context and his own historical moment to the universality of the Christ event. Paul connects with the larger intention of God's love transcending space and time and personal circumstances.

> *...but it has now been revealed through the appearing of our Savior Christ Jesus, who abolished death and brought life and immortality to light through the gospel....*

Notice the flow back to the historical event that provided the connection between the everyday human drama and the ultimate divine overture of union.

...for the Gospel I was appointed a herald and an apostle and a teacher, and for this reason I suffer as I do....

Paul identified another cause of suffering and does so correctly. God did not call him to suffer but to serve, and often it was his apostleship that exposed him to the afflictions he would endure.

...I know the one in whom I have put my trust and I am sure that he is able to guard until that day what I have entrusted to him.

In this final expression of the contemplative dimension of his faith Paul offers up himself and his future even unto the end of time.

Other saints have echoed Paul's sentiments. St. Teresa claimed suffering had become sweet to her because of the overriding joy of Christ's presence and love in her agonies. So focused was St. John of the Cross on love and union with God that he was able to write a major portion of the Spiritual Canticle while starving and imprisoned in a tiny, lice-infested cell.

We are called to witness to the same strength that God has provided through the ages. Ours is a collaborative ministry that finds its own rhythm of speaking and listening, acting and being, moving forward and stepping back, confronting and nurturing. The caring minister knows suffering, faces it, names it, exposes it to the light, and applies love to it in lavish amounts. Our struggles, when met with courage and trust, become the most significant profiles of Christ's ongoing resurrection power.

"And remember, I am with you always, to the end of the age."
(Matt. 28:20)

The Grace to Say Goodbye

Little children, I am with you only a little longer. You will look for me; and...now I say to you, "Where I am going you cannot come." (John 13:33)

I will not leave you orphaned; I am coming to you. In a little while the world will no longer see me, but you will see me; because I live, you also will live. (John 14:18–19)

Jesus came and stood among them and said, "Peace be with you." (John 20:19)

When the pastoral caregiver enters into the life of someone in crisis it can be in the midst of a life-changing "goodbye." The care receiver may have lost a loved one, a career, a role, or health. The transition has forced the person to walk through a door, leaving one life behind to face the unknown. Life is a series of hellos and goodbyes. The caring minister becomes the companion along the route of recovery and represents the family of faith and God's tangible presence. Times of grief must be gone through to allow life to take shape in a new pattern. Goodbyes can mean new beginnings.

It will be necessary at some point to make a definite shift in the caring ministry relationship, to put some closure on the ministry that has served its purpose. This is going to require some care on the part of the caring minister and consultation with your pastoral care team or supervisor. Saying goodbye is always difficult, but not doing so and simply fading out of a person's life causes much more pain and hurt and can unravel all the effective ministry that has taken place. Closure of the caring relationship is as important as anything you do.

Once again we turn to Jesus as our model for skillful ministry. He approached his necessary "goodbye" to those he loved with clarity, compassion, and celebration.

Clarity

"Little children, I am with you only a little longer."

When Jesus knew it was time to bring his earthly ministry to a close, he was very clear and honest with his followers. His honesty was difficult for them to swallow; when Peter tried to dissuade Jesus, he was quickly rebuked. Denial would not be on his path, and in the long run facing reality would prove to be a kindness.

For the caring minister clarity of purpose and availability will be addressed at the very outset of the association. The pastoral care supervisor should set some norms for the care receiver prior to the initial meeting. The supervisor needs to spell out the unique function of a caring minister and perhaps even estimate a time frame for the commitment. For example:

SUPERVISOR: "I've discussed this with Maryann and she is able to meet with you for the next six to nine months."

The caring minister, by words and actions, will reinforce the unique character of the relationship by keeping it focused on caregiving and spiritual sharing. Closure will be easier to introduce if the caring minister has been clear about boundaries and limitations along the way. Don't take on responsibilities that are going to encourage dependency. For instance, if an elderly homebound care receiver asks you to grocery shop on a regular basis, you would be wise to put that person in touch with a supermarket that provides a delivery service.

Throughout the relationship be assertive about your availability.

CARE RECEIVER: "May I have your number at work so I can call you if I need to?"

CARING MINISTER: "That really won't work well with the nature of my business. You may leave a message on my home voicemail, and I'll return your call when I'm able to."

The goal is not for the caring minister to become a good friend of the care receiver but rather a primary pastoral resource during a time of difficulty.

When it becomes evident that a care receiver is well on the road to recovery, the caring minister takes the initiative in exploring closure. Ending the caring relationship is not going to be accomplished in just one session. When you sense that it is time to look at ending the formal association, meet with your pastoral care supervisor to discuss the reasons for closure and how best to go about it.

Usually you will approach the subject with the care receiver by reviewing the person's progress:

CARING MINISTER: "You've made so much progress since our first meeting."

CARE RECEIVER: "Oh, I know, but I can't do it without our weekly visits."

In this case the difficulty is still spoken about in the present tense. The care receiver is still receiving important encouragement and support from the relationship, and it is too soon to taper off the visits.

CARING MINISTER: "You've made so much progress since our first meeting."

CARE RECEIVER: "Yes, I don't know how I could have made it without our weekly visits. It was so reassuring to know I would be seeing you on Thursday afternoons."

In this case the care receiver is able to reflect back on the initial crisis: it is referred to in the past tense. The caring minister might now suggest meeting less often. The caring minister receives clarity from the responses and reactions and needs to proceed accordingly. This is not a process that needs to be rushed.

Compassion

"I will not leave you orphaned."

Jesus did many things to ease the pain and desolation of the ones he left behind. It's impossible to imagine the account of the resurrection without Jesus' various appearances. Each encounter was a caring and compassionate communication that eased the despair of the grief-stricken community. Jesus gradually reduced his presence, and each appearance fortified the disciples' faith, turning what they thought to be the end into a new beginning.

"Because I live you also will live."

Jesus' life and intimate association with his followers made a difference. Jesus didn't just leave them; he left them with something. They were changed and strengthened by the relationship. They would savor his words, remember his teachings, and gain new insights in his absence. Yet he did not leave them orphaned. His spirit would continue to connect them with the divine source that could never abandon them.

Caring ministers model Jesus' ministry by gently taking their leave at the appropriate time and in a compassionate manner. When a care receiver begins to demonstrate signs of recovery, the pastoral caregiver needs to begin to back out of the picture and encourage the newly acquired self-esteem and reliance on God to emerge.

Among the signs of recovery are when the care receiver:

- cries less often;

- rehearses the events of the crisis less often;

- begins to do new things, for example, a woman recently widowed learns to do the taxes;

- demonstrates assertive behavior, for example, a man laid off from a job begins to make new contacts and writes a new resume;

- refers to the future with hope;

- is reflective about new spiritual insights;

- can talk about the loss without becoming paralyzed by the feelings (this doesn't mean a person never cries).

The caring ministry relationship creates a legacy for both the caring minister and the care receiver. Both are changed by the relationship and both receive a gift from sharing in a sacred time of grief. Closure of the relationship can put both in touch with the mystery of going forward after a loss.

Celebration

*Jesus came and stood among them and said,
"Peace be with you."*

During Jesus' final appearances the disciples were already beginning
to show signs that they realized the broader implications of his ministry, death, and resurrection. They were coming into their own;
they would continue Jesus' ministry with new power. Their witness to the resurrection and ascension would begin a new church,
and the cycle of dying and rising would be the central theme of
religious celebration.

The final meetings between the caring minister and the care receiver can be a time of celebration and blessing. "Goodbye" is
derived from the expression "God be with you"; it is a farewell blessing that imparts the message, "do not be afraid, God goes before
you, you are not alone."

When it is evident that the care receiver is ready for the formal
relationship to end, you will still need to exercise patience and sensitivity. In most instances a deep friendship will not develop. If it has it
should be made clear that you will no longer be this person's caring
minister but rather now look forward to a friendship. In cases where
a friendship has not developed, it is necessary to have a final visit
and establish the nature of ongoing involvement. For example:

CARING MINISTER: "I've been so blessed by our meetings as I've
witnessed your healing process. I'm glad that we'll still see each
other at church and be able to talk from time to time."

At the final visit review the events and reflect upon strengths, insights, and paths of new direction. This is also an opportunity for
caring ministers to share how they have been blessed and nurtured
by the times spent together. Ritualizing the "graduation" with a
small gift (for example, a mug or a book) leaves a tangible symbol
of healing for the care receiver.

After closure has taken place the caring minister may wish to remember the care receiver at holidays or on an anniversary of the
death of a loved one. However, this is entirely the decision of the
caring minister. Above all practice love, patience, and compassion in
this process.

Conclusion

We who have collaborated on this little book hope that it has contributed to your understanding of pastoral care and to your continuing faith formation. If in any way it has renewed your appreciation of Scripture reflection and the central focus of Jesus Christ as the one who reveals God's good intentions toward the world, then we are blessed and thankful. Now go. God is with you as you reach out to others in Christ's love.

Finally, beloved, whatever is true, whatever is honorable, whatever is just, whatever is pure, whatever is pleasing, whatever is commendable, if there is any excellence and if there is anything worthy of praise, think about these things that you have learned and received and seen... and the God of peace will be with you.
(Phil. 4:8–9)

Spiritual Application

"If a shepherd has a hundred sheep, and one of them has gone astray, does he not leave the ninety-nine on the mountains and go in search of the one that went astray? And if he finds it, truly I tell you, he rejoices over it more than over the ninety-nine that never went astray." (Matt. 18:12–13)

I was on retreat at the convent at St. Walburga's a few springs ago, and I especially enjoyed watching all the new baby lambs and mothers graze and play. All the ewes that year had twins, which were nice and plump. But my attention was drawn to three orphaned lambs significantly smaller than the others. The smallest of the three could barely walk and was usually off by herself sleeping or just watching the activity of the other sheep around her. She had been stepped on at birth and was not expected to live, but the shepherd wanted to give her a chance at life and so she intervened. I would sometimes go to the fence to pet the baby lambs who would run over to greet me. Even the little sick one would make it over on her wobbly legs. But once they all got a whiff of me they would quickly lose interest and walk away. I was not the shepherd; they couldn't recognize me and knew I had nothing to offer that they needed. In the evening the shepherd arrived to lead them from pasture to barn. They all ran to greet her, even the ewes and the robust lambs. They recognized her, she was their caregiver, their provider and protector. She scooped up the littlest lamb in her arms and the others followed her to their nightly destination.

One evening I asked the shepherd why the other ewes didn't care for the little orphans, especially the wounded one. She looked at me with surprise wondering, no doubt, how I had missed the obvious. She explained to this ignorant city girl, "They each have twins and have more than they can handle." The fate of the orphans depended entirely on the shepherd.

That is an image I shall always carry with me when I read a Good Shepherd passage. It was clear that those sheep knew and trusted and eagerly followed the shepherd who deeply cared for their well-being. From our childhood we've all been influenced by the tenderness of Jesus and the image of him going off to look for the one lost lamb. It evoked in us the awareness of God's individual and very personal concern for each one of us, and it is an important aspect of our relationship to God.

Ministry, healing, and recovery most certainly take place in the context of a nurturing community. Yet no one person can provide all that we need, be present at every moment, or suspend the loneliness that grips the heart in the night hours. There is a place of deep communion where we venture alone, although to say we are "alone" with God is something of an oxymoron. We can never truly be alone. God's being is expressed in the community of the Trinity, and God's nature requires that the Great Shepherd be attached to us with tender, steady, unshakable presence.

Contemplative prayer cultivates our knowledge and recognition of the shepherd. The more intimate and regular the encounter, the sharper one's "hearing" becomes to the voice that leads to paths of wholeness.

We are empowered to shepherd others, and our ability to be strength for others will depend, to a great extent, on how well we follow Christ. Do we do the things that nurture our identity with Christ? Do we recognize the voice of our caring God? And for that matter, is our identity so established that when harmful things cross our path are we able to take a whiff and determine, "That's not the Shepherd, that will not provide me with strength or growth, that is not compatible with my deepest calling in God?"

For your final reflection exercise, begin with a slow reading of Psalm 23.

- Now think back to a pivotal faith experience in your life. It may be one in which you discerned a course of direction or received strength from within for a difficult task.

- Recall your feelings, intuitions, insights

- How did you know they were from God?

- What confirmation did you receive from others or from circumstances?

- Reread Psalm 23 and use the imagery to take you to the secluded place in your heart where God speaks to you alone. Linger and be refreshed.

- Let go of all imagery, feelings, thoughts, and insights, and allow the Shepherd to speak to you in silence.

๛ Appendix

The Method of Centering Prayer
by Thomas Keating

Theological Background

The grace of Pentecost affirms that the risen Jesus is among us as the glorified Christ. Christ lives in each of us as the Enlightened One, present everywhere and at all times. He is the living Master who continuously sends the Holy Spirit to dwell within us to bear witness to his resurrection by empowering us to experience and manifest the fruits of the Spirit and the Beatitudes both in prayer and action.

Lectio Divina

Lectio divina is the most traditional way of cultivating friendship with Christ. It is a way of listening to the texts of Scripture as if we were in conversation with Christ and he were suggesting the topics of conversation. The daily encounter with Christ and reflection on his word leads beyond mere acquaintanceship to an attitude of friendship, trust, and love. Conversation simplifies and gives way to communing, or as Gregory the Great (sixth century), summarizing the Christian contemplative tradition, put it, "resting in God." This was the classical meaning of contemplative prayer for the first sixteen centuries.

Contemplative Prayer

Contemplative prayer is the normal development of the grace of baptism and the regular practice of *lectio divina*. We may think of prayer as thoughts or feelings expressed in words. But this is only one expression. Contemplative prayer is the opening of mind and heart — our whole being — to God, the Ultimate Mystery, beyond thoughts, words, and emotions. We open our awareness to God, whom we know by faith is within us, closer than breathing, closer than thinking, closer than choosing — closer than consciousness itself. Contemplative prayer is a process of interior purification leading, if we consent, to divine union.

The Method of Centering Prayer

Centering Prayer is a method designed to facilitate the development of contemplative prayer by preparing our faculties to cooperate with this gift. It is an attempt to present the teaching of earlier time (for example, *The Cloud of Unknowing*) in an updated form and to put a certain order and regularity into it. It is not meant to replace other kinds of prayer; it simply puts other kinds of prayer into a new and fuller perspective. During the time of prayer we consent to God's presence and action within. At other times our attention moves outward to discover God's presence everywhere.

The Guidelines

I. Choose a sacred word as the symbol of your intention to consent to God's presence and action within.

II. Sitting comfortably and with eyes closed, settle briefly and silently introduce the sacred word as the symbol of your consent to God's presence and action within.

III. When you become aware of thoughts, return ever so gently to the sacred word.

IV. At the end of the prayer period, remain in silence with eyes closed for a couple of minutes.

Explanation of the Guidelines

I. "Choose a sacred word as the symbol of your intention to consent to God's presence and action within." (cf. *Open Mind, Open Heart*, chap. 5)

1. The sacred word expresses our intention to be in God's presence and to yield to the divine action.

2. The sacred word should be chosen during a brief period of prayer asking the Holy Spirit to inspire us with one that is especially suitable to us.

   a. Examples: *Lord, Jesus, Father, Mother, Mary;* or in other languages: *Kyrie, Jesu, Jeshua, Abba, Mater, Maria.*

   b. Other possibilities: *Love, Peace, Mercy, Silence, Stillness, Calm, Faith, Trust, Yes;* or in other languages: *Amor, Shalom, Amen.*

3. Having chosen a sacred word, we do not change it during prayer period, for that would be to start thinking again.

4. A simple inward gaze upon God may be more suitable for some persons than the sacred word. In this case, one consents to God's presence and action by turning inwardly to God as if gazing upon him. The same guidelines apply to the sacred gaze as to the sacred word.

II. "Sitting comfortably and with eyes closed, settle briefly and silently introduce the sacred word as the symbol of your consent to God's presence and action within."

   1. By "sitting comfortably" is meant relatively comfortably; not so comfortably that we encourage sleep, but sitting comfortably enough to avoid thinking about the discomfort of our bodies during the time of prayer.

   2. Whatever sitting position we choose, we keep the back straight.

   3. If we fall asleep, we continue the prayer for a few minutes upon awakening if we can spare the time.

   4. Praying in this way after a main meal encourages drowsiness. Better to wait an hour at least before Centering Prayer. Praying in this way just before retiring may disturb one's sleep pattern.

5. We close our eyes to let go of what is going on around and within us.

6. We introduce the sacred word inwardly and as gently as laying a feather on a piece of absorbent cotton.

III. "When you become aware of thoughts, return ever so gently to the sacred word."

1. "Thoughts" is an umbrella term for every perception including sense perceptions, feelings, images, memories, reflections, and commentaries.

2. Thoughts are a normal part of Centering Prayer.

3. By "returning ever so gently to the sacred word," a minimum of effort is indicated. This is the only activity we initiate during the time of Centering Prayer.

4. During the course of our prayer, the sacred word may become vague or even disappear.

IV. "At the end of the prayer period, remain in silence with eyes closed for a couple of minutes."

1. If this prayer is done in a group, the leader may slowly recite the Our Father during the additional two or three minutes, while the others listen.

2. The additional two or three minutes give the psyche time to readjust to the external senses and enable us to bring the atmosphere of silence into daily life.

Some Practical Points

1. The minimum time for this prayer is twenty minutes. Two periods are recommended each day, one first thing in the morning, and one in the afternoon or early evening.

2. The end of the prayer period can be indicated by a timer, provided it does not have an audible tick or loud sound when it goes off.

3. The principal effects of Centering Prayer are experienced in daily life, not in the period of Centering Prayer itself.

4. Physical symptoms:

   a. We may notice slight pains, itches, or twitches in various parts of our body or a generalized restlessness. These are usually due to the untying of emotional knots in the body.

   b. We may also notice heaviness or lightness in the extremities. This is usually due to a deep level of spiritual attentiveness.

   c. In either case, we pay no attention, or we allow the mind to rest briefly in the sensation, and then return to the sacred word.

5. *Lectio divina* provides the conceptual background for the development of Centering Prayer.

6. A support group praying and sharing together once a week helps maintain one's commitment to the prayer.

Extending the Effects of Centering Prayer into Daily Life

1. Practice two periods of Centering Prayer daily.

2. Read Scriptures regularly and study *Open Mind, Open Heart.*

3. Practice one or two of the specific methods for every day, suggested in *Open Mind, Open Heart,* chap. 12.

4. Join a Centering Prayer support group or follow-up program (if available in your area).

   a. It encourages the members of the group to persevere in private.

   b. It provides an opportunity for further input on a regular basis through tapes, readings, and discussion.

Points for Further Development

1. During the prayer period various kinds of thoughts may be distinguished (see *Open Mind, Open Heart,* chaps. 6–10):

   a. Ordinary wanderings of the imagination or memory.

   b. Thoughts that give rise to attractions or aversions.

   c. Insights and psychological breakthroughs.

   d. Self-reflections such as "How am I doing?" or, "This peace is just great!"

   e. Thoughts that arise from the unloading of the unconscious.

2. During this prayer we avoid analyzing our experience, harboring expectations, or aiming at some specific goal such as:

   a. Repeating the sacred word continuously.

   b. Having no thoughts.

   c. Making the mind blank.

   d. Feeling peaceful or consoled.

   e. Achieving a spiritual experience.

3. What Centering Prayer is not:

   a. It is not a technique.

   b. It is not a relaxation exercise.

   c. it is not a form of self-hypnosis.

   d. It is not a charismatic gift.

   e. It is not a para-psychological experience.

   f. It is not limited to the "felt" presence of God.

   g. It is not discursive meditation or affective prayer.

4. What Centering Prayer is:

   a. It is at the same time a relationship with God and a discipline to foster that relationship.

   b. It is an exercise of faith, hope, and love.

   c. It is a movement beyond conversation with Christ to communion.

   d. It habituates us to the language of God, which is silence.

Bibliography

Alcoholics Anonymous. 3d ed. New York: Alcoholics Anonymous World Services, 1976.

Arnold, William V. *Introduction to Pastoral Care.* Philadelphia: Westminster Press, 1982.

Becker, Arthur H. *Ministry with Older Persons.* Minneapolis: Augsburg, 1986.

Boykin, John. *The Gospel of Coincidence.* Grand Rapids: Zondervan, 1986.

Fairchild, Roy W. *Finding Hope Again.* San Francisco: Harper & Row, 1980.

Feil, Naomi. *The Validation Breakthrough.* Baltimore: Health Professions Press, 1993.

Holmes, Urban T., III. *Spirituality for Ministry.* San Francisco: Harper & Row, 1982.

Hunter, Robert L. *Helping When It Hurts.* Philadelphia: Fortress, 1985.

Johnston, William, ed. *The Cloud of Unknowing.* Garden City, N.Y.: Image Books, 1973.

Keating, Thomas. *Intimacy with God.* New York: Crossroad, 1995.

Keating, Thomas. *Open Mind, Open Heart.* Warwick, N.Y.: Amity House, 1986.

Keating, Thomas, and Gus Reininger, eds. *Centering Prayer in Daily Life and Ministry.* New York: Continuum, 1998.

Kornfeld, Margaret. *Cultivating Wholeness.* New York: Continuum, 1998

Kübler-Ross, Elisabeth. *On Death and Dying.* London: Tavistock, 1969.

Lewis, C. S. *The Screwtape Letters.* New York: Macmillan, 1961.

Nugent, Robert. *Prayer Journey for Persons with AIDS.* Cincinnati: St. Anthony Messenger, 1989.

Raphael, Beverly. *The Anatomy of Bereavement.* New York: Basic Books, 1983.

Reimer, Lawrence D,. and James T. Wagner. *The Hospital Handbook.* Wilton, Conn.: Morehouse Barlow, 1984.

Schultz, Karl A. *The Art and Vocation of Caring for People in Pain.* Mahwah, N.J.: Paulist, 1993.

Teilhard de Chardin, Pierre. *The Divine Milieu.* New York: Harper Torchbooks, 1960.

Van Kaam, Adrian. *Looking for Jesus.* Denville, N.J.: Dimension Books, 1978.

Vanstone, W. H. *The Stature of Waiting.* New York: Seabury, 1983.

Westberg, Granger E. *Good Grief.* Philadelphia: Fortress, 1962.

Williams, Earle and Elspeth. *Spiritually Aware Pastoral Care.* Mahwah, N.J.: Paulist, 1983.